He Ain't Heavy... He's My Brother

Guns, Girls & Gambling in East Texas

Rocky D. Hawkins

Cover and interior design by
Crystal Wood/Tattersall Publishing; photos courtesy of
the author and his family, and are used by permission

Printed in the U.S.A.

ISBN 979-8620-735815

Note: The following memoir is based upon actual
persons, places, and events as recollected by the author to
the best of his memory and/or related to him by persons
named herein. Any factual errors, omissions or exclusions
are entirely unintentional. Though many of the anecdotes
included in the narrative describe alleged illegal activities
and persons who may have engaged in them, the persons
so named and justly convicted have long ago paid
their debts to society. No harm or disrespect is meant
to any person, living or dead, nor to their relatives or
descendants.

Dedication

I dedicate this book to my precious wife, Laura, who has loved me, forgiven me, and stood by me through it all for over 35 years. "I love you beyond words."

And to my two sons, Jesse and Daniel. "Thank you for never giving up on me. I love you and am so very proud of you both."

Acknowledgment

Thanks to Laura Beth Louvier for assistance with copy editing and development.

I owe much gratitude to Crystal Wood for her expertise in bringing clarity and focus to this account of a "long road with many a winding turn," and for her skill in preparing it for publication.

Introduction

The term "dysfunctional family" never showed up much until about the 21st century. This became the new buzzword for when some nut-job is caught in bad behavior and claims injustice. Any psychological, emotional or physical problem a man has can now be traced back to and blamed on his "dysfunctional family."

Back in the 1950s and -60s, I wouldn't even have been able to pronounce the term. Little did I know that I was living smack-dab in the middle of one.

A man can make a lot of excuses for the mistakes he has made. I have penned these short escapades, not to make excuses, but to help with the healing. I think it might just be working.

Rocky D. Hawkins
May 2015

Foreword

"If Hawk liked you, you had a friend for life. If he didn't, he was subject to hit you over the head with a cash register."
— Ernest Harper

"If Hawkshaw tells you that Santa Claus is coming on the 4th of July, don't ask any questions, just hang up your stocking."
— Lacey Lovell, TABC, Longview, Texas

"I always thought Hawk was in the poultry business. Every time I talked to him he was headed down to 'the Chicken Ranch' to pick up some money."
— Kenny Roberts

"Me and my brother got in a scrap over a pool game when we were kids. Hawk threatened to whip us both with a wet squirrel if we didn't settle down."
— Reggie Hawkins

"Sometimes, the truth is a hard story to tell. The beginning of Rocky's book was great, but the ending was even better."
—Harold Wells, Mayor, Gladewater, Texas

"There is a fine line between truth and fiction, and I think I snorted it somewhere in 1979."
— Kinky Friedman

Chapter 1

Until I was about forty years old, it seems my life was always centered around an old falling-down beer joint, Bar-B-Q joint, "cat house," or alcohol of some kind.

My dad was a "two-time loser," who looked like Marlon Brando and fought like Al Capone. He could whip most men, grabbin' at 'em.

He never made a showing at Mother Francis Hospital in Tyler, Texas the day I was born in 1952. He was running a crap game for Curtis Duke at the Shady Grove in Kilgore, Texas. My dad, James Hawkins AKA Hawkshaw, started floor-bouncing for Curtis when he was about nineteen or twenty. This was an old hay dock/block building that seated about sixty people. Curtis and Hawk set up a crap game in the back and busted many a roughneck and pulpwood hauler out of their paychecks.

Hawk was a pretty good "dice mechanic." He could "kill a six" on every roll. He learned how to roll one die and spin the other without it turning over. He would shoot out of a cup and check the numbers before every roll. This increased his chances of making his "point" by about 70 percent. Not bad odds for an old scuffler. He later on said "killing a five" was better odds.

All you needed was the right kind of spots on the dice, and it was pretty easy to separate the suckers from their money. Most of them didn't like losing, so they got a good "spankin' " too, if they tried to get their money back.

Hawk probably won a couple hundred thousand dollars before he turned twenty-one. Lots of green for back in 1952.

Curtis was really a pretty nice guy. I got to know him a little after I got older. He was one of the few men ever to get paroled out of Alcatraz Federal Penitentiary. He showed me an overcoat he was really proud of that was made by "Machine Gun" Kelly there in the sewing factory. When things got slow in the "joint business," Curtis would get on the road for a few weeks at a time to hustle up some cash.

He might rob a poker game out in West Texas, or pick up a load of "hot cigarettes" to resell with no government tax stamp. Curtis had all kinds of scams to make money. He had a liquor store right next to the Shady Grove. I used to call on this account when I worked at the Budweiser Beer Distributorship many years later. He carried me out back one day, and rocked an old car body with a Thompson submachine gun he had confiscated on a debt somebody owed him.

But Curtis was not the first con-man to turn Hawk out. It was really his stepdad, Buster Holley, or Uncle Buster, as we called him. He was Tessie Lou's second husband. Uncle Buster was a great guy, and loved me and

Curtis Duke's ticket
out of Alcatraz.
Very few of these
were ever granted.
(See enlarged
versions in
back of book.)

Baby Reggie with "Uncle Buster" Holley, Tyler, Texas, 1949

my brother. He hauled us many a mile in an old 1954 Dodge he called "Heaven Dust." He had no children of his own.

Buster was the original con-man who came out of the Depression. He sold Bibles and straight pins door-to-door, bootlegged whiskey, and taught Hawk how to shoot craps.

One scam he told about was selling "bug pads." They were strips of cardboard that were dipped in melted-down mothballs. They were fifteen cents apiece. "Guaranteed" to kill mosquitoes, flies, bugs, and all kinds of flying insects for farmers, fishermen, and children.

When Hawk was about twelve or thirteen, he and Buster would sell half pints of whiskey to the soldiers when the train would stop at the depot in Tyler, Texas. Because Tyler was dry, and the whiskey cost $5 a pint, they made lots of quick cash during the War.

One time Buster bought a truckload of shoes to resell. All of these were left foot shoes only. It was all you could get during the War.

Buster promised to buy Hawk a '39 Mercury convertible if he finished high school. Hawk quit the next day, and hit the road. Hawk's parole officer once said that Hawk had an

I.Q. of 125. Hawk always said it was too much trouble to go to school.

Hawk finally did get his G.E.D. while he was at Leavenworth, in 1962, and threw it in the trash on the way out the door.

Buster used to make my brother and me go into the grocery store and ask for "free give-away" papers to roll his own cigarettes from a Bull Durham sack. He never smoked what he called "ready-rolls."

Uncle Buster's most famous quote was, "Two people can keep a secret, if one of them is dead." Another of his favorite sayings was, "When they were handing out noses, I thought they said *roses,* and I asked for a big, red one."

Buster had a small morphine habit, but I heard he kicked it on his own in a flophouse, right off the square in downtown Tyler. It took forty-eight hours of fighting the demons, but he got the monkey off of his back for good.

Chapter 2

Hawk and Curtis had beat a rancher out of $2,500 and got a lot of heat from it. I think his son was William Wayne Justice, District Judge from Athens. He put the cops on Hawk's trail. Hawk carried my mom and Curtis to Havana, Cuba for a couple of weeks until the heat was off.

I'm not sure when Hawk got into the "girl" business. He called the girls "the Rackettes." Most people called it plain ole pimpin'. It was just too much for my mom. She was a good Baptist girl, and didn't want any part of it. She lit out and carried my brother and me with her. I was less than a year old, and my brother, Reggie, was about three years old.

A couple of years later, she married a long, tall, drink of

Our mother, Mattie Bell (Bement), and father, James Hawkins, on their honeymoon in Havana, Cuba, 1947.

water named Travis. He was making a living driving a truck. Travis was okay, but he couldn't handle his liquor. Even though neither my brother or me had red hair, we took our share of "scoldings" from Trav, and his ole Mexico belt.

What we did like as we got older was Travis' oldest boy from his first marriage, Mike. Mike was the ultimate "Fonzie" from the 50s. He grew up in Dallas with his mom and was a few years older than my brother, Reggie. He had hair like Fabian and was cool as well water. He taught us all about roll and pleat seat covers, tear drop headlights, 4-bar flippers and spinner hubcaps.

He turned us on to Wolfman Jack's radio station, and taught us how to smoke grapevines. Tokin' on a piece of wood was tough on your lungs and made your tongue feel like sandpaper, but man, it made us the Star of the Show in Athens, Texas in 1959. I think Mike ended up in a shootout with the Highway patrol. He couldn't handle his liquor, either. Mike was a great artist, guitar player, and quite the ladies' man.

I remember listening to guitar licks with him by Duane Eddy; the song, "Pipe Line" by the Chantays was a great

*Hawk and
Mattie Bell, 1948*

*Travis and Mattie Bell
with their "4-hole" Buick, 1956*

*Hawk and a
1939 Mercury*

tune we liked to listen to. Mike told us all about *Hot Rod Magazine*. We would put the magazine covers in our "view through" notebooks at school. He taught us how to "spit polish" a pair of shoes with paste wax and set them on fire to set the shine. When he finally left town, we were all wearing St. Christopher medals around our necks, and smokin' them grapevines. He was the best, Jerry!

Chapter 3

I remember one summer Reggie and I spent in Kilgore, Texas, at a nice, family, roadside court called Rogers' Motel. Pop Rogers ran this dump, and Hawk had his working girls on location there. It had about twenty cabins full of junkies, prostitutes, and drunks—a very wholesome (?) environment for two boys, five and seven years old. I remember Reggie mixing drinks for some ole drunks under a shade tree in the afternoons. A couple of characters I remember was a lady named Mojita, and an ole cement mixer named Shorty Wright. I think they were drinking Carstairs whiskey and Coke.

My grandmother, Tessie Lou, was working on her third husband by this time. He was a really nice guy named Bill Riggs. "Mam-Maw" knew better, but she was an ole scuffler like Hawk and was always waiting on him to make his next "Big Score."

Tessie Lou had a tattoo on both arms, and could go toe to toe with any man in a knock-down, drag-out. She was good as gold to Reggie and me, and loved us unconditionally. There was a lot of Indian blood in that side of the family,

Agnes Odessa Coley,
AKA *Tessie Lou*

Tessie Lou,
AKA *"Mam-Maw," 1958*

and it would leak out when they lost their temper. If you have ever heard Al Dexter's hit song, "Pistol Packin' Mama," from 1943, listen for the verse about a girl named Tess. Her given name was Agnes Odessa Coley, but everyone called her Tessie Lou or Tess.

I wish I had spent more time with her after I got older. She bought the farm at about 64 years of age. Too many Lucky Strikes, I guess!

Money got tight, and the heat was on, so it was about this time that Hawk hit the road for Dog Patch, Oklahoma. Dog Patch was a spot in the road, just across the state line in Oklahoma. One of Hawk's gangster friends had told him about an old sawdust honkytonk for sale. Hawk got the "fix" on with the local sheriff and set up shop. Hawk told me later that it cost $40 a month for the sheriff to let him run wide open. Tessie Lou and Bill Riggs moved in to help run the place. His main bartender was a guy named T.D. Southern. I remember T.D. had a stray dog named "Loopy." He would chase his tail out on the dance floor in front of the jukebox.

His wing man was Cliff Caughman. He knew the rackets, and was good with his fists. He still lives in Hot Springs, Arkansas. I heard he got saved, joined a church and struck it rich in the construction business.

*Tess on the right,
with little James Hawkins*

This whole part of Oklahoma was dry, and Hawk had no sign of a liquor license. I must have been about five years old, but I remember a back room behind the bar, where Hawk kept his bootleg whiskey. There were a couple of 2x6 panels in the wall that could be slid back to reveal a great hiding spot for a couple of dozen half pints of Old Crow whiskey.

The whiskey flowed freely, the crap game was set up in the back, and the jukebox blared out front. Hawk was making money with both hands. My brother and I would come visit in the summer and on holidays.

There were a couple of trailer houses on a hill behind the joint where we stayed. I remember Hawk having a full-grown chimpanzee in a cage out back. This chimp hated women for some reason, and would spit and scream any time a woman would come near the cage.

Leta Jo Coley with James "Clifton" Hawkins holding
baby Joe Charles Kelly

Isn't it funny what things a five-year-old remembers about his childhood? I remember one holiday we spent in Dog Patch, when Hawk showed Reggie and me how to place a firecracker under a Vienna sausage can and flip it up into the air! I saw Tessie Lou grab a live chicken and sling it around by the neck until its head popped off. She cleaned it and cooked it right on the spot. Exciting stuff for a kid to see.

Hawk was in his prime, ten feet tall and bulletproof, when things got a little too hot to handle. He had girls working a spot in Tulsa. I found a good little article in the *ABA Law Journal* that gives a pretty good summary of Hawkshaw's downfall, after this trip to Tulsa.

I don't think the "Mann Act" is still on the books, but it bought Hawk his first two-year vacation to Leavenworth Federal Penitentiary.

Hawkins *vs.* United States
Doc. #2

Hawkins was committed under the Mann Act for driving Lola Fay Mindy, age 17, in his orange Cadillac with the leopard-skin upholstery from Dog Patch, Oklahoma, to Tulsa to work as a call girl for his estranged wife, Jane Wilson. En route, Hawkins crossed into Mena, Arkansas, to get a headlight fixed.

Hawk got him a "nickel" for this stupid mistake, but the Supreme Court later reversed the conviction, upholding the "Spousal Privilege" that a wife cannot testify against her husband. Leavenworth cut him loose after about two years.

Tessie Lou took me and Reggie to visit Hawk a couple of times in Kansas. It was pretty scary for an eight-year-old boy to walk up the steps of a federal penitentiary. All of the locks, bars, and guards were a lot to deal with. After we declared who we were, and who we wanted to see at the guard tower, I remember climbing a giant flight of concrete stairs to the entrance. A guard led us in to a holding area that had a big, grey, steel door. Behind that was a set of prison bar doors that opened into the visitation room.

See *James Clifton Hawkins, Petitioner v. United States of America*: https://law.resource.org/pub/us/case/reporter/US/358/358.US.74.20.html

Federal prison is not like the State. You don't make contact by telephone through a glass window. We went into a room that had four tables that were separated by a bench on one side and chairs on the other. My brother, grandmother and I sat in the chairs. A few minutes later, a guard led my dad into the room to see us. He was seated on the opposite side of the table. There was no physical contact after the initial greeting. Pop was dressed in prison blues, not black and white stripes like you see in the movies. All the other inmates were dressed just the same. The only thing that was different were Hawk's shoes. His cellmate had hand-painted some white stitches around the soles of these big ole brogans to look like expensive dress shoes. We all got a big laugh out of that.

Overall, the visit was pretty sad. We stayed about four hours. The trip had taken about fourteen hours from Kilgore, Texas. I am pretty sure I saw a tear in the corner of Hawk's eyes when we hugged good-bye.

Not long after Hawk made the trip, another tragedy struck our family. Hawk's second wife, a lady named Ermaleen, was killed in a car accident. While out partying with a bunch of Hawk's friends, the car ran off the road and up an embankment; Ermaleen was thrown from the car, and killed with a broken neck as the car rolled on top of her. This proved to be a huge controversy in Hawk's life of "settling the score." Some say it was a man named Sonny Lacy driving the car, but others say it was someone else. I guess we may never know the real truth.

I remember two federal agents bringing Hawk into the funeral wearing handcuffs. It was shameful for even a con man and his family. The feds had brought him down from Kansas to pay his respects. This event led to his transfer to the Federal penitentiary in Seagoville, Texas, near Dallas. This was a minimum security prison for non-violent offenders. We made several visits here. A couple of these were with Uncle Buster. The visitations were a lot more lenient here. I remember having lunch outside in a gated

Ermaleen Hawkins is buried in the Mt. Pisgah Cemetery in Wood County, Texas

area with picnic tables for the families. Hawk said, "the back fence has been trampled nearly all the way to the ground by cons jumping the fence for conjugal visits with wives and girlfriends."

I am pretty sure it was while he was at Seagoville that Hawk got busted for D.W.I. while on a work detail. Somebody had made some "hooch" from fermented potatoes, and left it for Hawk in a fruit jar. It was discovered by the guards in Hawk's possession and cost him thirty days in the "hole" (solitary confinement), and a transfer to Texarkana. Hawk said this unit was a "hog farm." The Federal Correctional Institution of Texarkana was hard work and low pay. We made a couple of visits here, but I don't remember much about the place. Hawk was not here too long before he made parole. On a "nickel" sentence, I think he did two and a half years.

Somewhere along the way, my grandmother had ended up back in Kilgore, Texas, running a joint outside of town called the "Tessie Lou Club." It was located where the movie theater and car dealerships are now. My brother and I spent a couple of great summers around this ole honky tonk. We were still living in Tyler during this time. I think I counted up about ten to twelve elementary schools that we attended while growing up.

Travis was a carpenter/painter by now, and we moved anywhere he could find work. Many times I remember moving during the night, about the time the rent was due. Momma would say, "Don't tell anybody we are moving." We must have moved about a hundred times before I was in the sixth grade. Travis was a hard worker, but never had any credit or ever saved a penny.

We never owned a new car, a telephone, or had air conditioning when we were growing up. We ate beans 'n taters, fried bologna, potato patties, and pickle-loaf sandwiches. We had fried chicken occasionally, but never asked for seconds, and never tried to snack after supper. What was left over was for the next day!

Like I said before, Travis was a good guy. His biggest problem was that he had no self-esteem. He had dropped out of school early on, and joined the navy. The man served in World War II, but unfortunately got a D.D. (dishonorable discharge) from the military for going A.W.O.L. chasing after his first wife. He came home to Tyler on leave, and didn't return back to his base on time. This D.D. was tough on a résumé! Travis was pretty much self-employed as a painter and carpenter our whole lives.

His temper always got the best of him on about every job he ever had. He tried to get Reggie and me to quit school in about the sixth grade, and go to work with him. He said you didn't need much schoolin' after you could read and write. I remember Hawk sayin' that Travis was quite a scrapper. Hawk said, "He would jump on Tarzan." Travis was about six feet two inches, and weighed about 165 pounds. He always wore cowboy boots.

One of my fondest memories growing up, was a trip to the local grocery store we all made during this time. The family car was a beat-up, old 1947 Plymouth that Travis was going to "fix up." Mom and Travis were in the front seat, and Reggie and I were in the back. When we got ready to leave the store, the old dog of a car would not crank. Back then, sometimes, if you pumped the gas pedal several times, it would prime the carburetor, and help it to start the car. The carburetor ended up getting flooded—and Trav got a "Charlie Horse" in his leg. He was "madder than a Jap"! He reared back and proceeded to stomp the windshield out of the car! My brother and I were moon-eyed in the back seat, shaking all over! Travis climbed out of the car to walk off the Charlie Horse and to cool off a little.

When he got back in the car, it started up on the first try. Good story now, but we were a couple of scared rabbits at the time. I just remember that Travis' eyes looked like two burnt holes in a blanket. Mattie Bell had already had her ears boxed for nothing, and I knew we were next. I can't imagine what Momma was thinking.

"Matt" and Trav had a son named Dwain. He was my half brother and a good guy. He could never get his life on track. His life came to an end in the Smith County jail on New Year's Eve 1977. He O.D.'d while "huffing" Right Guard deodorant. What an awful circumstance for my mom to go through!

After Trav and my mom got married, we moved to Farmer's Branch near Dallas. We lived in a falling-down rent house that had no indoor plumbing. We still had an outhouse in 1956. We lived pretty rough during this time.

I remember one Christmas at this place, that my brother and I got a "Swamp Fox" coloring book (they cost about 10 cents each), and we got a variety 64-pack of crayons (which we had to share), from Santa Claus. Not a very big Christmas for two boys!

Another not-so-pleasant memory of this place was when Reggie and I were burning trash behind the house when I backed into the flames and caught my britches on fire. I started running for the house—this was before "stop, drop, and roll" was invented. Reggie tackled me and beat the fire out with his hands. Momma came out the back door screaming and took my pants off outside. A little piece of my skin came off with the pants. I remember her doctoring my burns with black salve. She never took me to the doctor—no money!

It seems like we left here and headed for Carrollton, Texas. This was where I started the first grade in school. Travis had scored a job driving a truck. We lived in a ratty little frame house, but the neighborhood had a lot of friends to play with. We learned how to go "craw-daddin'" and jump off the roof with a towel around our necks like Superman. I think it was here that Mam-Maw bought us a bicycle. It was lots of fun, and I think Travis rode it to the grocery store a couple of times when his car was broken down. Later on, our bikes got stolen by the neighbors.

We went to the drive-in theatre for the first time when we lived here. Saw *Old Yeller*—about the best movie ever made.

The Christmas we spent here was another "best." Travis was gone on a truck run. Momma had found a very small tree, about two feet tall, and placed it on the coffee table. We decorated it with some old broken beaded necklaces. Travis came in on Christmas Eve and had bought us a couple of novelties he had found at a truck stop. I got a wooden roadrunner toy. His head bobbed up and down when he drank from a glass of water. I think Reggie got a coonskin cap—good stuff!!

Travis had a bad habit of punching Mattie Bell around when he got to drinkin'. After a couple of black eyes and a string of bad luck in the trucking business, we headed out to Corsicana, Texas.

Travis and Momma had cut a deal to move in with her sister, Billy Jo, and my Uncle Boyd. This had disaster written all over it!

We loaded up everything we owned in the back of a pickup, and left in the middle of the night. We never checked out of school or even told the landlord. The plan was to share the rent and Travis and Boyd would go into the remodeling business together. We moved into a big ole shack with a long porch, and bedrooms on each end with a shared kitchen in the middle. Travis and Boyd drew a blank in their new business venture. We all nearly starved early on.

I remember Boyd climbing a telephone pole to turn on the electricity, and opening the water meter at the curb to turn on the utilities without the city knowing it.

We raised rabbits and chickens in the back yard for a while. Rabbit is not bad when it is cooked just right. Guess what it tastes like? Still, we had fun when we lived there!

Boyd had two kids. Dennis, who was my age, and Judy, who was Reggie's age. Dennis and I were in the first grade, and Reggie and Judy were in the third. We would all walk to school and back every day. There were a couple of antique stores with a lot of junk in the yard, and we would stop there on our way home every day. Dennis showed me a wooden airplane propeller that he found there that was pretty neat. There was all kinds of junk for a kid to explore.

Sometimes we would stop at a fruit stand on the way home and buy an apple that cost ten cents. We would shine it on our shirt-sleeve before we gnawed down on it.

I loved my cousin, Dennis. He was a daredevil, and fairly shameless, even in the first grade. I remember him jumping over a little rock wall one day on the way home from school, and "dropping a load." Just like his dad, Boyd, he never wore underwear. I didn't think much of it at the time; just something that needed to be taken care of.

I remember one time, Dennis and I got busted at a Safeway store after school. We were killing time, waiting for Reggie and Judy to get out of school, when Dennis spotted a couple of cases of Coke bottles behind the store. He grabbed one and busted it against the back wall. I joined in the fun, and before you knew it, all the bottles were shattered all over the parking lot. Just one of the stupid things kids do without thinking of the consequences. The manager came out and made us clean up all the glass, and threatened to tell our parents. I'm not sure if that ever happened, but Dennis sure knew how to get into mischief.

It seems like I am putting all the heat on Dennis, but he is the one who grabbed a pack of Old Gold cigarettes from his mom's purse and taught us how to smoke. We would hide under the house —a big ole "pier and beam"—and puff away. None of us knew how to inhale the smoke, but we sure could puff on those Old Golds. About the third time we went to our hiding spot, Billy Jo found us, and hollered for Travis and Boyd. Dennis and I took off running for town. Reggie was left behind. They said Boyd had a rubber hose in his hand for a belt to whip Dennis. Travis had his big ole "Mexico belt"!

We all ended up back at the house about sundown for a "Big Smoke Out"! Even though all the adults in both families smoked, they were determined to teach us boys a lesson. They made us sit down on the floor in the kitchen, Indian-style. Travis gave us all a package of Camel cigarettes. Reggie, Dennis, and I had to smoke the cigarettes, and every time we didn't swallow the smoke, we got a lash across the legs with a belt. The punishment was "Smoke until you puked." After about three drags and three lashes, Reggie was the first out the back door. I was next, and we were in the back yard heaving up our toenails. Dennis was the last to fall. He coughed a couple of times, spit, and thumped a smoke over the fence. Dennis was bad, baby—even in the first grade!

Dennis taught us how to burn bugs with a magnifying glass, and how to make a slingshot out of a forked tree limb. After we got a little older, Den-Den scored a Mo-Ped motorbike that we all took turns riding. Dennis knew some stuff!

Dennis hit a rough spot at the end of the first grade. He got the three-day measles, and Billy Jo let him stay home for three months. Seriously, he failed the first grade because he had missed so much of the year!

I can hear Billy Jo right now hollering for Dennis to come in on Sunday nights to take his "school bath"!

Judy was a little older, but she was fun, too! She showed us how to get into the Saturday morning kiddie show for free. We only lived a few blocks from town. They would run specials for kids every Saturday. Judy showed us how to check the pop box at the gas station across the street every day after school. We would run to the service station, and the guy that owned it would let us empty the bottle-cap container on the "you pull it" Coke machine. For six Sun

Drop bottle caps, you could get in the show for free. We saw some great movies: *The Shaggy Dog, Zorro, The Little Rascals, The Blob*, and all the Tarzan movies.

There was an ice cream company right across the street also. One afternoon a delivery truck parked right in front of our house. It was a hot day in July, and Dennis looked at me, and I looked at him. Quicker than a wink, he jerked open the back door of that truck, and pitched 2½ gallons of strawberry to me. We high-tailed it behind the house. Reggie, Dennis and I ate our weight in ice cream. I am not sure, but I think Reggie even barfed a little from all the ice cream!

Judy and Dennis had a rough upbringing. They were the ultimate dysfunctional family! I found out when I got older that Uncle Boyd was a little "partial" to Judy, and he was always threatening to kill Billy Jo. I heard Matt and Travis say one time they overheard Boyd threatening to cut her throat on the stroke of midnight. You could hear through the walls of that ole house, and the courthouse had chimes that rang at every hour! Boyd laid in the bed with a knife to Billy Jo's throat, and made the threat. Uncle Boyd never meant any harm; he just wanted to show Billy Jo who was boss.

Billy Jo was next to the youngest of five sisters. She had lots of emotional problems—no thanks to Boyd. When she was about eight years old, she stuck a nail in her foot on the way to the outhouse. The thing got infected, and ate a hole clean through the top of her foot. Momma said the doctor put maggots inside the cast to eat out the infection and dead skin.

One of the things I remember about Billy Jo is her shoes. They are called flip-flops now, but back then they were known as "shower shoes" or "go-aheads." Billy Jo got her a bright yellow pair and wore them for years! Those must have been her only pair of shoes while we lived in Corsicana. You could read the paper through the soles of those shoes when we moved.

We all hit the road for Athens, Texas in 1959. It seems like we lived in every rent house in Athens. Travis and Uncle Boyd had landed a job in the construction business, and was working out of a place called Willeford's Lumber Yard. We ended up living next door to Boyd and Billy Jo in a little neighborhood of frame houses that the Willeford brothers contracted out to Travis if he would paint it, and tape and bed it also.

Reggie, Dennis, and I had some great adventures the two years we lived there! There were two things Dennis loved to do. One was digging a hole in the ground, and the other was building a fire. We did a lot of both!

It was nothing for three or four kids from the neighborhood to get together and dig a six-foot square hole in one afternoon. You could throw a car hood over the top and make a great fort. Then you could spend the rest of the day having dirt clod fights. Nothing is worse than getting hit in the eye with a big ole dirt clod. Our hair and clothes would be filthy! It was huge fun! I remember a red-headed kid named Benny. We kept him captured all afternoon under the hood in a six-foot hole. Every time he tried to get loose, we would bombard him with big ole clods of dirt. He cried like a baby until we finally let him loose.

I remember one night that Dennis had a giant fire built in a field behind his house. We had been poking in it half the night when I had found a huge cardboard tube that was used to store linoleum in. For some bizarre reason, I thought I could insert this tube into the fire, and get a real close look. Fire and smoke singed off both of my eyebrows, and part of my hair. You know what burnt hair smells like? It was awful!

One thing we had fun doing was looking for muscadines (wild grapes). We would climb a tree in a minute to get to a cluster of mucadines. They never seemed that sweet to me. They are kind of thick-skinned with a seed in the middle. I do know one time I had climbed out onto a limb for a big bunch of grapes, and I busted loose a nest of yellow jackets. By the time I had run the half mile to the house, I had both eyes swelled shut, and knots all over my head from bee stings. I kind of lost my appetite for muscadines after that.

We would ride our bikes for miles in the summer, picking wild plums and chinquapins. Man, those little suckers were hard to find! We thought they were delicious, but they really looked and tasted like acorns from an oak tree. A lot of times, Uncle Boyd would load up us kids in an ole junk car, and take us to the "clay pits" to go swimming. These were really rock quarries, that were deep blue and ice cold. Man, we had some fun! These were located "across the tracks," because as best I can remember, there were always lots of black kids swimming with us. Uncle Boyd was fearless!

Uncle Boyd had given Dennis a spelunker's headlight for his birthday. It was really a spotlight with a headband on a three-cell battery that hooked to your belt. We couldn't wait to try it out.

Not too far from the Athens Elementary School was the city's main rain water drainage system. In the Spring, we would fish for crawdads here, but in the summer, it was pretty dry. It had a huge concrete room that led to culverts and drainage systems all over Athens. For a couple of punks with flashlights, and a great spelunker's headband, we couldn't resist.

The concrete tunnels were pretty easy to maneuver at first. But the farther we went, the smaller they got. After about four hours, we ended up in a concrete tunnel about twenty inches wide. We had skinned backs and knees, and no room to turn around. Our batteries were getting weak, and nobody wanted to say they were scared, but everybody was; Reggie, Den-Den, and I. We finally found daylight about a mile and a half from where we started as we climbed out of a water drain on Highway 31 in front of a little country service station. We had holes in our jeans and blisters on our hands. We were mighty glad to see daylight! Many times I have looked back and given thanks to God for protecting me, and helping us get grown. We never knew what happened to Dennis' headlight after that.

This had to be around 1960, because Chubby Checker had just invented a new dance called the "Twist." Hawk was finishing up his stretch in Texarkana Federal Correctional Institution, and my grandmother was running a beer joint (the Tessie Lou Club) in Kilgore, Texas. This is where Reggie and I spent that summer.

We loved to visit Mam-Maw. She lived in a two-bedroom trailer behind the joint, and a little ways down a black-topped road. Man, it was great! She had cold air conditioning and a telephone. She would cook a huge breakfast for us on Sundays, and you could eat all you wanted. She was a great cook, and loved to cook for my brother and me.

She pretty much ran that ole bar night and day, so the City Swimming Pool and the Crim Movie Theater were our babysitters for the summer.

Kilgore had a great city pool that had a huge rock front, and blue water to die for. We spent many long hours swimming and playing here as kids. Fifty years later, it is still in business.

It was here that we met a guy named Neal Noel. This cat could swim and dive like Tarzan. Double back flips, jack-knives, gainers, you name the stunt, and he could do it off the high diving board. Sandy blonde hair and a big barrel chest, he looked like a movie star. I wish I had gotten to know him better, but he was always at the pool when we went there.

It was the pool during the day, and the Crim theatre at night. You could get a cab for seventy-five cents to drop you off right at the front door. Sometimes Mam-Maw would get one of her bar flies to haul us around. Many nights

Bill Riggs and Tessie Lou; Vernon Wheeler and wife; Bill and Leta Jo Neal at Tessie Lou's Lounge in Kilgore, Texas, 1958

The Neals with Toni and Hawk

we would just sit at the "Family Table" in Mam-Maw's old beer joint and listen to stories from her customers, as the jukebox blared songs of Jim Reeves, Hank Thompson, Eddie Arnold, and Kitty Wells. I can still hear Slim Harpo singing, "Rainin' in My Heart," and Fats Domino, "Walking to New Orleans."

Many nights Reggie and I would sit there watching those ole drunks dance the jitterbug. We would drink 7-Ups and play shuffleboard until closing time.

Tessie Lou was a great dancer, and knew how to hustle the jukebox. She would match customers a quarter because she would paint hers red with fingernail polish, and get it back when the jukebox man counted the money to check up the machines.

I can still smell the cigarette smoke and stale beer. Nothing like the aroma of floor sweep and dance powder they threw out on the dance floor. Hamm's beer had some great beer signs that lit up the back bar, along with great pool table lights. I remember Pearl beer, Budweiser, and Falstaff signs on every wall.

All of the bartenders and waitresses had nicknames for all the brands of beer. If they called out, "Ride one, slide one, and send one to school," they were ordering a Jax, a Schlitz, and a Budweiser. No mixed drinks were served. It was BYOB— bring your own bottle—and set-ups were served. I remember 7-Up bottles had a picture of a boy carrying his books; they called this set-up a "school boy."

I remember one waitress named Mary Dilly. She worked

Reggie, Rocky, and Junior playing shuffleboard at Tessie Lou's Lounge, 1958

At the 1963 State Fair of Texas: Bill Brewer, Rocky and Reggie

for my grandmother a long time, and was a good friend. We got to meet a lot of real characters at this ole joint!

I remember Mam-Maw pointing out a customer one night. She said, "That's Red Adair and his crew sitting over there in the corner." Red became world famous for having one of the first companies that fought oil well fires that were out of control.

There was one character that came by several times a week selling hot tamales. All that I ever knew about him was that his name was Cooper. He would walk in the front door of that ole joint hollering, "Cooper's Hot Tamales! Cooper's Hot Tamales!" Those things were delicious!! They cost one dollar a dozen or ten cents apiece. These things were hot and greasy and came wrapped in newspaper. Man, we ate tons of them that summer!

Cooper drove an ole beat-up car with a Prestone Anti-Freeze can screwed to the top of his car. I never got the connection. Years later, someone tried to say Cooper sold a few pills on the side. If his can was standing up, he was in business. I used to see his car all around Gladewater and Kilgore even after I got in high school.

Most every weekend there was a photographer who would come in to take pictures of men and their wives, girlfriends, etc.—anyone out for a good time. The Polaroid camera had just come out and you could get your picture right there on the spot. The negative would appear right before your eyes. Man, it was like magic! Everybody called this guy "Hollywood Wally." He was about five feet tall and had a gimp leg. He made all the joints in town. He must

*Toni, Hawk, Leta and Bill Neal;
with "Juan Moretime"
in Nuevo Laredo,
Mexico, 1964*

have made some pretty good money. Later on, I heard he got in a jam for trying to transpose someone else's head onto his pictures, and also for doing some blackmailing on the side. This was not good for business. I never knew whatever happened to Wally!

Reggie and I got to know the beer men on a first name basis. They came in three days a week to deliver beer, stock the cooler, and pick up long neck empties. They were all a bunch of great guys, working hard for a living.

One of the things that I remember about the beer was that it was all in steel cans back then. No "pop-tops." You would use a "church key," or bottle opener, to punch a hole in the top. One large hole, then turn the key around for a smaller hole. Most bars had a contraption on the counter that had a lever on it that you slammed down on the top of the can to punch the holes. Quite a souvenir if you could find one!

I remember the responsibility of the beer man was to collect poll tax for voters' registration. You could pay your dues at your local bar, and the beer driver would pick it up. This was an old law that stayed on the books until about 1965. It was designed to keep minorities from voting. I think it was $1.75-$3 to have the right to vote.

Who would have ever thought then that Reggie and I both would end up working our way through college at the Budweiser Distributorship in Longview, Texas, and later on Reggie would work for Ben E. Keith in Dallas? We learned a lot in the beer business.

Many nights after closing time, Mam-Maw would carry us to a place called the Shack Café. All of the bar operators would come down to this place about one in the morning to eat. Reggie and I played many hours on a great pinball machine that had a wooden bat for flippers. The grown folks drank coffee and ate chicken fried steak. On Sunday, they served a plate lunch "family style" for only seventy-five cents. This would sure get the ole wrinkles out of your belly.

Tessie Lou's was closed on Sunday. We might just end up at the Streamliner Restaurant or Albert's Mexican Village downtown for lunch. The Streamliner had yellow cream gravy and served a homemade miniature loaf of bread with every meal.

I remember sitting in the big red booth in the corner at Albert's. This was long before microwave ovens. The dinners were served in metal plates heated in a big ole oven. Albert's Mexican Village is long gone now, but you can still find his hot sauce coast to coast.

Chapter 4

It must have been about 1962 that Hawk finished his time at Texarkana Penitentiary. He came back in town "ready to rumble." He and Sonny Lacy tried to settle the score with the guy that was driving the car the night that his wife, Ermaleen, was killed. That man was chained to a tree, and almost beaten to death.

When the heat was on, he sold the Tessie Lou Club for $400, and he and Mam-Maw, and an ole gal named Leigh, moved to Plainview, Texas to cool out.

I know we spent one miserable Christmas up there. Hawk was flat broke, and we like to froze to death.

Hawk set up a front running a pawn shop while he and some guy named "Buzz" beat a few suckers out of their money in an ongoing craps game. Hawk finally made a score and set up shop in Dallas in about 1963. He rented an old spot on Carroll Avenue called Bud's Drive-In. We spent one of our best summers in this ole joint. It seated about fifty to sixty people, and had a big awning out front. Hawk installed a big swing out front for the car hops to swing and hustle customers. I am pretty sure this is where Hawk first got into the BBQ business. The old man he rented the building from already had a great pit, and showed Hawk the ropes.

I just remember this ole guy telling us stories about his boxing escapades. He really looked like Popeye: short, stocky, and had huge arms. He claimed he had gone ten rounds with Jack Dempsey back in the day. Hawk always claimed he was "punch drunk." Every time he heard a bell ring, he would start ducking and punching. All I know, is he had two huge cauliflower ears!

This place had a great jukebox, and a bumper pool table. By the end of the summer, we could beat any adult that came in. Elvis played on the jukebox, "Return to Sender" and Sam Cooke wailed out "A Change is Gonna Come." Gene Summers topped the charts with "Big Blue Diamonds." Still some of my all time favorite songs to this day!

Hawk put in a steam table, and put up a big sign that said, "Pitch Till You Win." This was a lunch bar, and it was all you could eat for seventy-five cents. Man, he packed 'em in at lunch!

Not long after Hawk got out of the Big House, he got a call from Ernest Harper. Ernest ran a liquor store out on the strip in Gladewater, and had been a friend to many a gangster over the years. He had heard about a gal from Kilgore that had lost her husband in a railroad accident. She had collected about $50,000 in his life insurance. Ernest knew just the man to help her spend her money!

He called ole Hawk, and a few days later, they "accidentally" met in an old beer joint in K-Town. The rest was history. She couldn't get to Dallas quick enough to invest in Bud's Drive-In, and the Talk of the Town Dress Shop right next door. She and Hawk spent money like a couple of drunk Jews. That year we all had a very Merry Christmas, to say the least.

I remember waking up about two o'clock in the morning, and hearing her and Hawk having a huge argument in the next room. The old man finally knocked her cold with a money sack full of change. A sack of quarters probably weighs about forty pounds. He said a wooden coat hanger would be next.

Hawkshaw really knew how to handle his women. She looked like she had on a Halloween mask the next morning. I have to say that she was good as gold to my brother and me. She bought Reggie his first car, a 1956 Dodge Coronette. This monster was green and white with a typewriter transmission. It cost $400 cash at Shugg's Auto Sales on East Grand in Dallas.

You have to remember, Hawk hadn't been home from the Big House long, and a bunch of his old cellmates followed him to Dallas.

Bud's Drive-In shared a parking lot with the "It'll Do" Club. I drove by a couple of years ago, and it is still there, and still in business. Bud's had changed names, but the building was still in the same spot.

The summer of '63 Bud's had a full clientele of pimps, bank robbers, con men, grifters, and gamblers of all makes and models coming and going seven days a week. There was Dugan Taylor, the "Big Hay Baler"; Big Tom, Little

The It'll Do Club (and this sign) is still in operation, but it's a very different music scene in Deep Ellum. Bud's Drive-In is now the Starlight Lounge.

Dave King, Henry Bowen, Jerry Ray James, and plenty of working girls to choose from.

We loved Dugan Taylor. He was an old-time scuffler from West Texas who smoked non-filtered Pall Malls and drank long-neck Budweisers by the case. The Big Hay Baler had drinking beer down to a fine art. He would tilt the bottle straight up (about half an inch) from his lips and pour it down his neck like water. He could knock out a cold one in about three swallows. I remember him having a cast on his leg for a while that summer. He was taking a little "cat-nap" in one of the back booths at Bud's when somebody dropped a live smoke down his cast. Dugan never opened his eyes—just poured about half a bottle of Budweiser down his cast and went back to sleep.

*Dugan Taylor (middle) with
T. D. Southern (right) at
the home of Ernest and Jewel Harper, 1965*

Dugan was at his best with a pair of "tops" dice. They had spots that shot only sixes and eights and never seven or eleven. They were best also for shooting "high dice." Reggie was about twelve or thirteen that summer when an old drunk stumbled into Bud's. Dugan used Reggie to con the guy into shooting dice for fun. Dugan stepped in with a pair of "tops" and cleaned the guy out of a couple of hundred bucks. The poor man started crying about losing his paycheck and Dugan told him to shut up or he would "kick all the hair off his head."

I heard many years later that the Texas Rangers beat Dugan to death with a coat hanger because he wouldn't rat out his friends in a bank robbery. Hawk had once told a story about the Rangers tying Dugan to a chain link fence and grabbing his testicles with a pair of channel-locks. I think Dugan spilled the goods like a drunk parrot before it was all over.

Big Tom looked like Dick Tracy—snap-brim hat, horn-rimmed glasses, and a full overcoat. He was a real ladies' man. Mainly because he kept plenty of "Black Mollies" and "West Coast Turnarounds" in his pocket. He said he could tie a pill bottle on a fishing line, cast it out onto the dance floor, and watch all the gals in the joint go wild! Big Tom had shared a cell with Hawk in Seagoville, and was mostly a safe mechanic, con artist, and front man for Jerry Ray James.

Little Dave never spent any time in the slammer, but he was a professional cat burglar, and would steal a hot cookstove. Dave looked just like Tab Hunter. He was real cool, always wore a sport coat, red Ban-Lon shirts, matching shoes and sunshades. You would think he

Hawk and Big Tom, 1964

was a stock broker from Dun & Bradstreet.

Hawk and Dave would buy their clothes on East Elm Street in Dallas at a shop that was run by a family of Jews. While Hawk kept 'em busy, Dave would make two trips to the car with socks and ties just for fun.

Dave got busted once taking Christmas packages out of a car at the Big Town Mall, but then talked his way out of it by claiming he had a car just like the one he was haulin' off.

Dave took pride in never paying a hotel bill. I think they call it "defrauding the innkeeper." Back then, hardly any credit cards were used; you paid your bill when you checked out. He could spot a Highway Patrol a mile away. We all went to Padre Island one year. Several families went in different cars. Dave took a dirt road about halfway there from Houston, and we didn't see him until we got to Brownsville.

*Hawk with Jackie and Little Dave
at Lake Tawakoni*

I didn't know it then, but later on, Dave would, literally, save my life. One thing Hawk and Little Dave had in common was fishing. Lake Tawakoni had just opened in Wills Point in 1963. Hawk was with that gal from Kilgore, Texas named Charlene, who had inherited that insurance settlement. Hawk had spotted a ski boat one evening on the way home from Bud's Drive-In, that was "for sale by owner." A couple of phone calls later, and we were the proud owners of a fifteen-foot blue and white Glasstron with a seventy-five-horse Johnson motor.

A couple of days later, Reggie, Hawk, Little Dave, Sonny Lacey and I were headed out to the tree tops on Lake Tawakoni for some crappie fishing. We were a good two and a half to three miles from shore, and it was about sundown. We tied off to a tree limb, and got our corks a-bobbin'. Hawk heard something that sounded like water

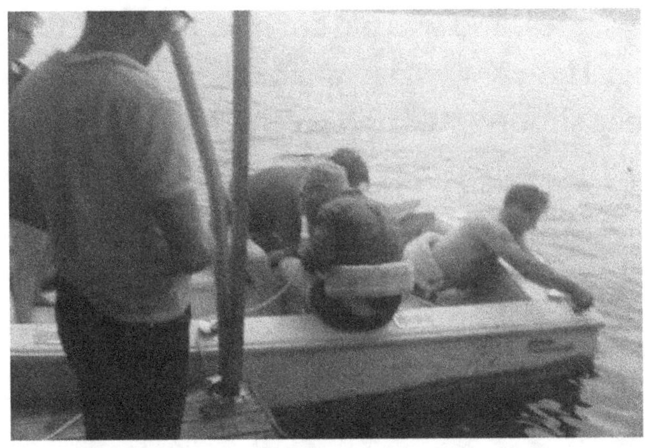

At Lake Tawakoni before the "shipwreck"

running. I was about ten years old, and Reggie was about thirteen. We didn't have a clue of what was going on. Hawk lifted up the back seat of the boat, and it was full of water. Within about five minutes, the boat was going down, and Hawk pitched Reggie and me up into a treetop. Sonny weighed about 350 pounds. He never even moved; he just reached up and grabbed a limb while the boat sank out from under him.

Hawk and Dave swam to some nearby tree tops. We hollered for help until we were hoarse. After about three or four hours, we spotted a barge about 500 yards away. Dave called the shot. Hawk had two kids to look after, and Sonny couldn't swim. Dave never backed up. He put on an old ski belt and swam from tree to tree, and came back a couple of hours later riding on that barge.

I've told that story a thousand times. Dave King will always be a hero in my book!! Many years later, Dave was killed in a private plane crash in Wichita Falls.

Henry Bowen had been in and out of jail most of his life. I think Hawk met him in Leavenworth. He was also a friend of Jerry Ray James, and was part of his safe-cracking, bank-robbing ring. Henry was also a stone-cold hit man. He once stated that shooting a man in the head was like "shooting a pumpkin off a fence post."

He ended up serving two life sentences for murder. Somebody said, "If Henry had gotten him a good lawyer, he could have gotten off of one of those."

Jerry Ray James was the nicest guy you could ever meet, but he was more dangerous than a den of rattlesnakes. He was famous for being quite the gentleman to all of the victims he robbed. He always asked if the ropes or gags were too tight for them. He always slept with a pistol under his pillow, and dated a black gal. He said, "That gal looks like a new saddle."

His specialty was doing a bank job on safety deposit boxes, even though he was never too particular as to how he made a quick score. While sitting at a bar in Dallas one night, a sucker pulled out a big bank roll to pay his tab. Jerry said, "What are you doing with something I need?" He robbed the man on the spot.

Once when he was holed up in a house in West Texas, he threw down a two-row shotgun on a couple of Texas Rangers. He said, "Y'all lay down in them grass burs, and drop your guns." He made it out the back door for a clean getaway. The man was fearless, and loved to mock any kind of law enforcement. He was very charismatic, and I heard that he started his own religion while he was in Leavenworth. He

---

See *United States v. Jerry Ray James*:
www.ecases.us/case/ca5/303180/united-states-v-jerry-ray-james

hated a "snitch," and things happened to those who crossed his path. One of his victims got hammered to death by a ballpeen hammer, and another one was burned alive in a garbage can. All this happened inside Leavenworth!

We were at the lake house in Gladewater several years later. I remember some high school buddies and I watching the late news one night when they showed the Ten Most Wanted list, and Jerry was number

Jerry Ray James was our houseguest one summer.

one. It said that he was known to be a smooth talker, a flashy dresser, and always wore red silk underwear. The kicker to this story: Jerry was asleep in the back bedroom at the time. He was running from the cops again and Hawk put him up at the lake house for a few days. We all went to Hurwitz's Man Shop the next day and bought us a half dozen pair of red silk drawers.

Texas Monthly ran a good article on Jerry a few years ago. It was about Jimmy Chagra, and the murder for hire conspiracy to assassinate a judge named John Wood from San Antonio. Charles Harrelson got blamed for the hit, but Jerry was a cellmate with Jimmy Chagra. Jerry Ray stunned his cronies by cutting a deal with the state and going into the witness protection program. He wore a wire with a microphone and tape recorder, and got Chagra to admit to setting up the hit on the judge. Jerry was doing a life sentence, and was desperate. He got the last laugh on the cops. *Texas Monthly* said it was a con job all the way.

Chapter 5

I don't know what Hawk was thinking, but he wanted Reggie and me to see him in action. I really think he was using us as a front, to promote his innocence and honest appeal. He and one of his dice mechanics had lined up a big crap game just outside of Dallas. The sucker ran a wrecking yard and loved to gamble. When we pulled up to his shop that morning, he had a crowd of men around him. He was showing how he could bend a tire tool! He could do it, and after that he bowed a couple of suspension springs "just for grins." This guy had arms like Charles Atlas.

Hawk's partner was dressed up like a country hayseed with overalls and a straw hat on. This guy was no "square John," but he looked like he just got shot out of a cannon. His job was to look like the lucky winner. Hawk set up a shoot-and-fade game and let the "farmer" win all the money. The plan was to take the heat off Hawk and they would cut up the money later on.

They played all day and half the night. The mark made several trips to the bank, but he lost several thousand dollars by then. Like a lot of desperate situations, this went from bad to worse in a hurry. Some ole "sweater" that was not even playing in the games commented on how many sixes and eights Hawk was hitting. The strong man grabbed up the dice before Hawk could catch him, and the jig was up. They started slamming down the overhead doors to lock ole Hawk up in the garage. He broke through a side door, and went out into the parking lot. The "farmer" broke for high ground and Hawk was on his own. He and the junkyard dog were kicking and clawing all over the gravel driveway. Hawk came out of his pocket with a .38 special and popped a couple of caps, and everybody got some air.

Somewhere in the scuffle, Hawk had given Charlene a large diamond ring for safekeeping. She shoved it down her bra and out of nowhere, the owner's wife cracked her between the eyes with a flashlight, grabbed the ring from Charlene, and took off running. Reggie, Charlene and I ran for the car. Charlene was blinded by all the blood that was running down her face, so Reggie jumped behind the wheel of Hawk's '59 Cadillac. Hawk had slammed the gate shut on everybody and taken off on foot down a dirt road. We drove up and down a lot of gravel roads half the night, but never found Hawk.

About midnight, we headed back to Bud's Drive-In. We no sooner got there, than Hawk showed up in a yellow taxi cab. He said he had cut across a pasture, and hoofed up on the Interstate, and then called a cab. He said he was carrying so much cash, he couldn't get his pistol in his pocket, and had lost it somewhere along the way. I am not sure how he kept the heat off after that little adventure, but he never cut the "farmer" in on his share of the winnings. What a summer for a couple of punks from Athens, Texas!

I remember one Saturday night when three couples came in to Bud's about midnight. All had been drinking quite a bit by the look of them. None of them ordered food, just beer. When Hawk cut out the lights about one A.M., this lively bunch was not quite ready to leave. One of the men asked Hawk, "Where do you live?" He was insinuating that he might make an unfriendly visit after closing time. Ole Hawk came around the counter with a meat tenderizer in his hand. This thing looked like a four-sided hammer! After a couple of licks on the head, some of them headed to the door. One of them ran to the bar and bent down to cover his head. Dugan Taylor cracked him in the backbone with a chrome napkin holder, and scolded the last one standing with a bottle of 7-Up. Dugan said, "He couldn't fade that 'school boy'!" By the time the cops got there, they were all stacked up out back like cord wood.

I have lain awake at night, wondering what kind of psychological impact this had on my growing up.

The demise of Bud's Drive-In was set in stone in November of 1963. President Kennedy was gunned down by Lee Harvey Oswald only a few blocks away. Hawk said, "Business died overnight!" The Feds were busting people right and left. They were questioning every person in Dallas that might have any kind of criminal record. Hawk locked the door on it, and headed to New Orleans.

He ended up running a bust-out joint owned by Carlos Marcello. I think Hawk ran a crap game wide open in this joint because the "fix was on." It was in this house of corruption that Hawk beat Fats Domino out of $2500 and a pair of gold cuff links.

He finally set up an inside robbery with a couple of guys named "Slim" and "Shorty." When Willie Nelson came on the jukebox singing, "Call it a night, the party's over," these two goons busted in and threw down on everybody in the joint. The next day, Hawk and his buddies cut up the money and Hawk headed to East Texas. After that summer, Reggie and I headed back to school in Athens with Momma and Trav.

The next summer, I had turned twelve years old, and that was the end of the line for Matt and Trav. My brother and I left home for good. At twelve years old, you could choose which parent you wanted to live with, and Hawk had the papers drawn up to take custody of us. We left Athens, and moved all the way to Gladewater, Texas, about sixty miles away.

Hawk was putting Mam-Maw back in business in a little wood frame building on the "strip" across the river in Gladewater. The business sold BBQ & beer. We moved to a room in the back. It was a little shotgun room behind a closed door to the café. Tessie Lou had a bed on one end of the hall and Reggie and I had bunk beds on the other end. We had a homemade shower made from a closet. "Tessie Lou's Lounge & Grill" – Home Sweet Home!

This was 1964, and Gladewater was booming. This strip of honky tonks was outside of the city limits, and ran wide open. Reggie and I would help cook the BBQ, wash dishes, and wait tables. Tessie Lou was head cook and bartender.

There must have been about ten or fifteen ole joints out there on the strip during that time. Almost all of the owners and bar flies would come by to eat at one time or the other.

The joints all had typical names: It'll Do Lounge, The Wagon Wheel, the Star Lounge, Blue Jean Club, The Hi-Ho Lounge, Eagle Drive Inn, The Green Frog, and Joe Hammond's Round-Up Club. There was a long line of liquor stores there also. Man, on Friday and Saturday nights, it looked like "Little Las Vegas" out there. There would be cars parked for miles on both sides of the road. Jukeboxes blaring, bands busting a note from open doors, people stumbling from one joint to another, There was always something going on out on the "strip." We saw more than our share of bar room brawls and car wrecks from our front row seat at Tessie Lou's. I watched my grandmother hold a man drawing his last breath, after he was hit by a car right in the middle of Highway 271.

This little moneymaker came to its demise at the end of the summer. It was a Sunday night, and Mam-Maw had closed early and walked to the Wagon Wheel, across the street. Reggie and I decided to cook us some tater-tots for supper before watching some Dick Van Dyke on the television in the back room. Reggie heard a noise, and thought someone was breaking in the joint. We crept up the hall and opened the door to the café, which we found engulfed by smoke and flames. We had forgotten to cut off the deep fryer! The exhaust fan had pulled the fire up into the walls, and it was nothing but kindling by this time. I ran next door to cut on the well pump, but the breaker was

The Green Frog Club, Gladewater, Texas 1956

off. There is nothing like water on a grease fire! We broke out the back door and met Mam-Maw in the parking lot and watched Tessie Lou's burn to the ground.

There was not a penny's worth of insurance, and everything we owned went up in smoke. Some ole drunk dropped his arm around Reggie and said, "At least you still have your health!" School started for us in Gladewater the next day.

Busted and disgusted, Ernest Harper gave us a place to stay in a little trailer house next door to his liquor store a few doors down the strip. We went to school smelling like smoke, and Tessie Lou went to work at the Green Frog Café. I sat at the counter and listened to Roy Orbison sing "Pretty Woman" on the juke box. What a way to end the summer!

Chapter 6

Gladewater, Texas had its own sordid past long before my brother and I arrived in 1964. When the oil boom hit in the 30s, it went from a spot in the road to roughnecks, road lizards, ruffians, and many hungry entrepreneurs from parts unknown. The town itself is located in Gregg County, about 120 miles east of Dallas, and about sixty miles from Louisiana.

Highway 80 ran east and west, while Highway 271 ran north and south. For many years it was an only wet spot between Shreveport and Dallas. There was a honky tonk, brothel, or liquor store on every corner. The Texas Rangers were called in many times to declare martial law during "Hot Oil" scandals, and all kinds of other illegal and ill-repute activities.

By the 1950s and early 60s, most of the beer joints had popped up outside of town, "across the river," and were still pretty wide open as far as the law was concerned.

Nobel Crawford was the sheriff of Gregg County, and king of the mountain when it came to taking care of business. If you took care of him, he would take care of

*A young Elvis Presley
played in Gladewater
at the Mint Club before
his career took off.*

you. If you were doing something illegal, he wanted to know about it—and business was good!

Many of the old honky tonks were made famous back in the day, when celebrities, early in their careers, would show up for one night stands. While Elvis was doing the Louisiana Hay Ride in Shreveport, he made several showings in G-Town. He played the old Mint Club with a three-piece band for $75 a night. Tom Perryman was a local disc jockey and promoter that worked out of KSIJ Radio Station. He brought Elvis to town several times.

The owner of the Mint Club (later known as the Star Lounge) was William Smith of Tyler. He said, "The hillbillies of East Texas didn't know what to think about Elvis. I know he brought the house down with one wild show that night. I think the cover charge brought in about $90." William's ex-wife, Erlene, is a good friend of our family, and she was at the Mint Club the night Elvis performed. (She and Hawk have done a little co-habiting off and on for the last 25 years.)

The great Johnny Cash wrote, "I Walk the Line," while passing through Gladewater. Some say he was making reference to the old strip of beer joints across the river.

The Red-Headed Stranger, Willie Nelson, has an album out that mentions the Green Frog Café outside Gladewater.

Like a lot of small towns, it has had its share of heroes and hopefuls. Most of the action outside of town came to a screeching halt when the fire chief was killed in 1968. An old, senile joint operator named Thad West went to sleep in the back of his bar with a lit cigarette. When the fire department showed up, the joint was in flames, and Thad thought someone was breaking in. He shot and killed Chief Potts on the spot. Thad got life in Huntsville, and the City Council passed enough regulations to put most of the beer joints out of business.

In 1964, Hawkshaw was on a roll. After Tessie Lou's burned down, he made a deal to lease the Blue Jean Club across the street. The jukebox companies and vending machine owners loved renting to Hawk. He would spend money fixing up the building and they would split the take from the machines.

Every joint had a pool table, shuffleboard game, pinball machine, and a jukebox. Hawk wrapped this old haddock building in pink neon. He slapped a new handle on the sign, and the "My O My" Club was off to the races. Hawk

The My O My Club was the jumpin' joint in G-Town in the mid-1960s, and convenient to Hawk and Spider Smith's used car business.

was bringing G-Town to the next level in the joint business. While Dallas and Shreveport had go-go girls for a while, it was a first for Gladewater. Hawk left the front door wide open, and Gladewater beauties in skimpy, fringe outfits and white go-go boots were stopping traffic in both directions.

Pulpwood haulers, roughnecks and rednecks filled up the joint every night. They came from Tyler, Lindale, Kilgore, and who knew where else. Hawk had his good buddy named, E.T. Charles, tending bar for him. "East Texas Fats" was an ex-M.P., and could roll a beer can fifty yards with a .45. He weighed about 300 pounds, and was "cat quick." Hawk said E.T. was the most dangerous man he had ever met. Fats got crossways with a couple of toughs from Dallas. He said, "You boys are too strong for me. Let me go outside and get my little brother." He came back in with a sawed-off two-row to settle the score. He knocked the bark off their heads and sent them packing. It was nothing to have three or four bar room brawls every night.

Hawk dragged a couple of trailer houses out back. He lived in one, Reggie and Tessie Lou and I lived in the other. Many mornings, we would catch the school bus right out in front of the My O My Club. The original "white trash," living large in G-Town! The characters Hawk ran with all had a colorful reputation!

Joe Hammond had bought the Round-Up Club from Curtis Duke in the late 50s. It was a big old sprawling dance hall right next door to the My O My, so we were neighbors when I was growing up. I remember Joe having a bad leg, and when he walked across the sandy parking lot he never left a heel print from his right foot. Somebody had heisted a produce truck, and brought Hawk a truck load of yellow onions for his BBQ joint. Hawk told the cook to carry a fifty-pound sack over next door and set in front of the Round-Up. Hawk said, "In case the cops come lookin' around, they will think old Step-and-a-Half Hammond was the culprit that hauled off the onion truck." That old story still gets a laugh after all these years!

Sonny Lacey was a three-hundred-pound creep thief and was one of Hawk's inner circle of friends for many years, the other two being Joe Ben Wolfe and E.T. Charles. Sonny was never one to back up from a bar room brawl, and could take 'em on two at a time. He had several brothers who gravitated to different levels of larceny back in the day; think there was Earl, Chuck (AKA "Thin Man"), and Gerald. All of them have passed on now. Sonny gave it up at the age of thirty-six.

The "Big Man" had himself a serious eating habit. I heard him say he didn't eat enough to keep a snake alive!

Hawk said, "Yeah, a boa constrictor—eats his weight in food every day." The Doctor told Sonny that if he didn't quit eating, it was going to kill him. Sonny said, "I'd rather be dead." I saw him chow down on a spaghetti feast one night right after he had his appendix taken out. He busted out his stitches and had to have Dr. Hart sew him back up with baling wire! It took eight men to carry Sonny to the grave. Hawk said, "They had to hire some professional mourners to come to the funeral."

The big man loved high school football. You could catch him about any Friday night at Bear Stadium, hanging on the fence with a sweat towel around his neck. Reggie sidled up next to him one night and said, "Fats, who's winning?" Sonny said, "Man, who's playing?"

Sonny's nickname was Griswald. Because of his career choice, he mostly worked at night. He loved going to the Cozy Theater during the day. He never cared what was showing, as long as the AC was cold. I saw him eat two hot dogs at the concession stand while he was waiting on the lady to fix him some popcorn. The big man could put away some groceries!

E.T. Charles grew up in G-Town, and was one of Hawk's closest confidants. He was bad to the bone, but was really funny and loved a good practical joke. He had a working girl on a spot in LaGrange at the world famous "Chicken Ranch" by the name of Dirty Foot Tommy!

When Hawk went to Leavenworth the second time, it was E.T. that helped me

E. T. Charles,
about 1985

out of several financial jams. Hawkshaw needed some new reading glasses, and a subscription to the *Tyler Morning News*. I never had a penny, because I was still in high school, so East Texas Fats came through like a champ—he would give you the shirt off his back.

I sat down with Sonny and Hawk one night at the Steak House Grill to eat supper. E.T. said he hadn't been eating at this establishment much since the black fry cook had passed out and fell over on the grill—they had to scrape him off with a spatula. I threw up a little in my mouth, and Sonny busted out laughing. I had just been "Fanged"!

The owner of the Steak House Café was a man named Hinkle Ford. He was a good guy, and a good businessman. E.T. said Hinkle's first wife had left him because he wouldn't wear his wedding ring. Hinkle had lost both hands in an oilfield explosion. The big man could keep you rolling all night!

He was kind of sweet on the receptionist at the local dentist's office, and I think she was liking him a little, too. He went in for a check-up one day, and he gave her a red rose to show his affection. He told her to put it in the refrigerator to keep it fresh. He went back a couple of days later, and told her the rose was artificial. She got "Fanged," too!

E.T. and Hawk rode many a mile together, and made a lot of money together. E.T. passed away in 2005 in a local nursing home. He had dementia, along with several other illnesses. The receptionist at the dentist's office carried him home and took care of him till he drew his last breath.

*Hawkshaw and
Joe Ben Wolfe
outside the
My O My Club*

Joe Ben Wolfe grew up in Kilgore, Texas. He and Hawk crossed paths through some mutual friends, and became life-long pals. Joe Ben was never in the rackets, but liked a taste of the wild side. He owned the Country Tavern on Highway 31. He came up with the recipe to put a honey glaze and brown sugar on his BBQ ribs. This put the joint on the map!

He sold out many years ago, but the "Tavern" now is world famous. It has been featured many times in *Texas Monthly* magazine. It even has a couple of pictures on the wall of George Bush, Sr. and Larry Hagman (J.R. Ewing from the T.V. series *Dallas*), having lunch there.

I saw Joe and Hawk stand out in front of the My O My Club one night, and cull out a whole carload of pulpwood haulers. Joe put a bar towel around his knuckles and knocked two of them down as they were getting out of their car. Hawk bounced a pool cue off the other two's heads, and they all got them some air! They couldn't get back to Grand Saline quick enough!

Joe had a small office behind the bar at the Country Tavern where he could take a nap and peek out the window to keep an eye on the place. Once he watched his waitress pouring beer for her boyfriend all evening. She never rang up a quarter in the cash register. Joe never said a word to her, just walked out back and threw a brick through the front windshield of her new Mustang. Don't mess with Joe!

Back in the late 60s, times were changing. Joe didn't much like change. He had a big oak tree out back where he sold beer and BBQ to his black customers. He had a heck of a business "under the tree." When a couple of these customers came inside for a beer, Joe helped them outside with a .38 special and a slapjack! They turned out to be undercover for the NAACP! Joe had to sell the tavern to stay out of the pen.

Joe Ben moved to a little grocery store near Lake Cherokee on the outskirts of Longview, Texas. He had BBQ, a few groceries, and plenty of conversation. Joe would offer a small line of credit to his "good customers." They were mostly roughnecks and hay haulers.

Somebody said, "Joe, what do you do when somebody don't pay their bill?" Joe said, "I just move it over to somebody else's account that will pay!"

When Hawk had his coming-home party after his last trip to Kansas, Joe was there, along with about a hundred other good friends. Most of us got subpoenaed to the Upshur County Grand Jury a few months later, when a guy named

"Rabbit" came up dead after leaving the party. There were about twenty of us sitting out in the hall upstairs at the court house. We watched a pretty good-sized female court clerk walk up and down the stairs several times that morning.

Joe looked over at me and said, "If that ole gal has to walk up these stairs one more time today, she is going to get galled!" Loved to hear Joe tell a good story! He is still kicking in 2014, but pretty sick with cancer. I think he is living with his son, and still maintaining.

Burl Dean Holliman owned a liquor store on Highway 271 for many years. He was an eccentric character with an anti-establishment personality. At one time he had accumulated over 150 "fightin' chickens." He was shipping game-cocks all over the United States and Puerto Rico. This was quite the lucrative enterprise. Although it was illegal to fight roosters in Texas, it was not illegal to breed and sell them.

Reggie got a gig working for Burl Dean one summer building chicken coops, and taking care of the "flock." Part of his pay one week included a Rhode Island Red Rooster with a broken beak. This bird had been quite a scrapper, but was put out to pasture by its owners.

Travis showed him how to file down the beak, and get this bird back in the ring. "Hack Beak" won a little backyard battle, so we figured he was ready for the big time. Brother loaded up me and my pals John Erwin and Jim McDowell the next weekend for the big showdown.

The fights generally took place out in the country near East Mountain, Texas. This was just a few miles north of Gladewater. Nothing too fancy, but a lot of money would change hands after every scrap. The fights would take place on Sunday afternoons. The fighters would bring their best birds, then draw a ten-foot circle in the sand, and the fight was on! Death would call the winner. The birds were paired off according to size and weight. A game rooster has a natural spur on each foot. The "handler" would place a metal gav, or blade, on the spur with a small leather strap. This was deadly for its opponent.

Reggie finally got his bird into the pit about the fourth round. My buddies and I put together $30 on what we thought was the winner. "Hack Beak" lasted about two jumps before he gave up his last breath. We whooped and hollered and cheered on the chicken, but it was over. We lost our money, and Reggie lost his rooster. We got out of the chicken business after that.

Later on, I heard that Burl Dean and an old quack from Houston tried to invent a metal plate that was surgically implanted under the rooster's wing and breast to protect it during the fight. This little scheme never got off the ground because the roosters kept dying after the surgery.

Chapter 7

Hawk couldn't resist expanding his business. He put in real pit BBQ and a used car lot, all connected to the My O My Club. He brought in a new partner to run the car lot. The guy's name was Spider Smith, from Gilmer, Texas. This dude could fix anything with a spark plug. He could break down an engine and rebuild it blindfolded. Reggie and I loved Spider! He was about five foot six inches, real wiry, and had blonde hair the same color as dishwater. He was Hawk's wingman for years. Before he hooked up with Hawk, he had been the lead mechanic in every car dealership in the area. He had built and raced dragsters all over East Texas.

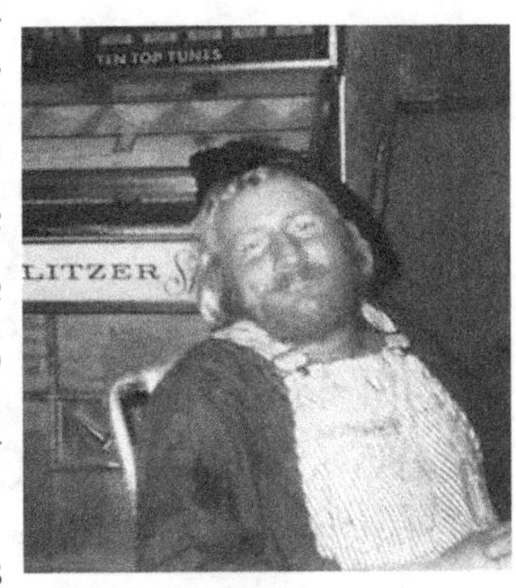

Spider Smith at Tuffy's Bait Camp Galveston, Texas 1973

His only problem was that he was weak for the ladies, and Hawk had plenty of them to spare. Hawk called the car lot "H & S Auto," for Hawk and Spider! He had a big sign painted across the front of the building saying "We Tote the Note." "We buy, sell, or trade – anything." We were living the dream! Hawk, Reggie, Spider, me, and anybody else that could drive were making runs to Art's Used Cars in Dallas. This ole nut ran a commercial in Dallas for a while, showing him knocking the windshield out of a car with a sledgehammer, hollering "I want to sell you a car!"

Bud Lansdale kept these old junk cars running for years. Bud was an ace mechanic, and had a garage right off of South Main Street, downtown Gladewater. There wasn't much he couldn't fix. (While Bud was infamous in his own right, it was his son, Joe, who really put G-Town on the map. A quick click on Google will give testimony to JoJo's success. He is a noted author, movie producer, and Karate expert extraordinaire.)

Hawk would buy an old clunker for $75-$100 and sell it for $50 down and $25 a week forever. If you missed one payment, Spider would hook onto it during the night and bring it back to the lot, ready to sell it again to the next sucker that pulled up.

A lot of times Reggie and I would drive anything that would crank to school. Spider was always up to a challenge when it came to mechanics. Hawk talked him into building a wrecker out of a 1958 Rocket 88. He cut it off at the front seat; tore out the back to the frame; installed a flat bed out of tank steel; put in an A-frame Stinger, and Gin Poll, and was ready for business.

Hawk was forever burning up the transmission in his old Caddies. Spider dropped a Hurst 4-speed with a

Corvette clutch into a '62 Fleetwood with no problem. We drove it all the way to Padre Island and back one summer.

Somewhere along the way, Momma and Travis ended up coming to Gladewater to help take care of my brother and me. Tessie Lou had bailed out and moved to Shreveport with her sister. Travis was going to help run the car lot, and do a little bartending on the side. Momma's job was to babysit the kids for Hawk's "working girls." He had girls working at the world famous Chicken Ranch in La Grange, Mama Nell's in Texarkana, and a little local business at Jackson's Motel in Longview. This had disaster written all over it!

I had the privilege of meeting Edna Milton, AKA "Miss Edna," the owner and madam of the Chicken Ranch, one afternoon in Gladewater. She was married to Glen Davidson. Glen was an old outlaw from G-Town. He had two brothers named Dingy and Daffy. We were all having lunch in the Hickory House BBQ on Highway 80. Mr. B.C. Woods was the proprietor. A girl about eighteen came in looking for a job. Miss Edna

"Miss Edna" Milton, owner/madam of the infamous Chicken Ranch, the inspiration for the musical "The Best Little Whorehouse in Texas"

looked up and said, "Why do you want to go to work in here, you're sitting on a million dollars." B.C. and I broke out laughing and the gal broke for the door.

This little setup lasted through the summer until Christmas Eve. Travis got left-footed drunk the day before Christmas and called Hawk out. Travis slapped Mattie Bell, and Hawk changed the color of his eye with one punch. Hawk called next door and told me and Reggie to get all the guns in the house, and put them in the trunk of his car. Travis was out for revenge.

Travis sobered up the next day, and packed up all he and Momma had and headed back to Athens. This was not one of our best Christmases. We all looked like we had been slapped away from the table for breaking wind that Christmas morning.

Reggie and I were on our own again. Hawk would bring in a couple of "bar room roses" from time to time to check on us, but we were pretty much flying solo. Hawk was spending a lot of time in Houston. He hooked us up with a $15-a-week charge account at Shaw's Fina Station for gas and lunch money when he was out of town. I was fourteen and Reggie was seventeen.

We had a saying in high school, "Some guys couldn't get a date at Jackson's Motel with a twenty-dollar bill!"

The My O My Club was jumping, the car lot was hopping, so Hawk decided to bring in the "girl business" too. He added a room on one end, decked out with plenty of red carpet, red and gold padded bar, and lots of girls. He had managed to get a private club permit through the

*Sandy Earp and some other colorful characters
with Hawk at the My O My Club, 1966*

Red Man's Association so he could serve mixed drinks. E.T. was tending bar and business was great. Hawk got a lot of heat from the locals, but he was out of the city limits, and had the fix on with the Gregg County Sheriff and the D.A. Hawk decided to bring in a sixty-foot trailer house a few steps out the back door for the girls. He painted the windows black, put a bathroom in each end, hung up a red light, and was in business.

My brother and I lived in a trailer right next door. It was not unusual at all to have some guy looking for the girls to knock on our door at two in the morning. Hawk was pimping out loud! It was out front of this ole joint that Hawk almost met his Waterloo.

He and E.T. had just boxed an ole roughneck around and thrown him out of the front door for being rude to the ladies. They were standing out front getting some air, when the guy jumped in his car and headed down the strip out of town. About ten minutes later he came flying back towards the joint, and unloaded a .32 caliber pistol in Hawk and E.T.'s direction. Hawk took a bullet in the chest, and he and E.T. dropped down on one knee and opened fire on the vehicle that was nearly out of sight by then. E.T. piled Hawk in the back seat of his ole Cadillac and headed to Hart's Clinic in Gladewater.

Dr. Hart took care of all Hawk's girls. He had them have a checkup once a week. Hart's Clinic was a one-man operation with about twelve rooms. Hawk had a punctured lung, and was bleeding internally. He stayed in the hospital about three days, where he almost died. He was drowning in his own fluids. E.T. broke him out during the night, and he and a nurse friend carried him to Dallas where a specialist put a tube in Hawk's back and drained his lungs. This saved his life, but every time he has an x-ray now, the lead bullet still shows up.

After a few weeks, it was back to business as usual. Hawk brought in a couple of "card mechanics" from Houston to set up a bust-out game in the back room of the My O My. This was really like something out of the old speak-easies in the 1920s! The men's room was at the end of a long hallway in the back of the joint. Hawk had a fake wall built in the end of the hall that opened up into a game room. It looked just like Vegas! It had a crap table with a Las Vegas lay out, and a couple of blackjack tables. Every time a poor old sucker came down the hall to take a leak, they would crack the door open, and let him see in. Temptation always won out.

It was like "The Sting" with Robert Redford and Paul Newman. Everybody was in on the deal but the drunk. The cards were marked, and the craps were loaded. Hawk brought in a couple of pretty girls and bam, before you knew it, another sucker was separated from his money. It was a smooth operation. It looked like you had winners and losers, but Hawk always ended up with all the money. These guys from Houston were hotter than a depot stove!

I saw Hawk get in an argument over a $5 bill with a man when the dude tore the bill in half, and Hawk whacked him across the ribs with a cam shaft, and also with a quick pop to the eye. The man hit the ground, but came back up and kept shooting craps. He looked over at Spider and said, "Is my eye swelling?" Spider said, "No, but your lip looks just like a beef heart." This was life in the fast lane!!

A few days later, Hawk and Joe Ben Wolfe had caught a couple of thugs trying to steal a set of hubcaps from the car lot. After they got through scolding him, Joe Ben dragged him under a car so he could back over his legs, but the car wouldn't crank. Joe was a big ole redheaded brawler from Kilgore. He was stronger than hemp rope. A lot of people don't know it, but this was the same Joe Ben who owned the Country Tavern and started the World Famous BBQ Ribs recipe.

Chapter 8

Hawk used an old counterfeit money scam over the years. He would get a bundle of new, crisp, $20 bills from the bank. He would flash them around until a sucker "took the bait," telling him, "You could double your money—two for one!" When the con came down, Hawk and a buddy would carry the "con" to Laredo, Mexico, or maybe Matamoros, across the border—"out of the country." The sucker would put up $2,500 and Hawk would put up his $2,500. The meeting would take place in a boot shop (the back of the bar). The Mexican connection would meet and take the cash, promising to return with $10,000 in counterfeit twenty-dollar bills after a few hours. The "runner" never returned. Everybody got "burned" and had to leave the country. Nothing you could do because it was all illegal and outside the U.S. The catch: Hawk had the "fix on." He had prearranged the "runner," and Hawk made off with the con's $2,500 and got back his own $2,500. No questions asked. There never was any counterfeit money!

P.T. Barnum, (Barnum & Bailey Circus) said, "There's a sucker born every minute." Hawk could spot one coming from a country mile.

Somebody said, "Hawk had more wives than Brigham Young!" I remember seeing Hawk knock an ole "bar fly" out the back door of the My O My Club with a stick of firewood for giving him a good cussing for getting her husband liquored up the night before.

One afternoon Ricky Hodges and I were putting an 8-track tape player in his old Dodge. We went by Hawk's to borrow a drill. An old drunk had stumbled into the trailer house out back by mistake. Hawk pulled a chrome, sawed-off shotgun from under his front seat, and popped the guy upside the head with the barrel. Ricky turned white as a ghost. We lit out without the drill and saw the drunk trying to hitch a ride to town holding on to one ear.

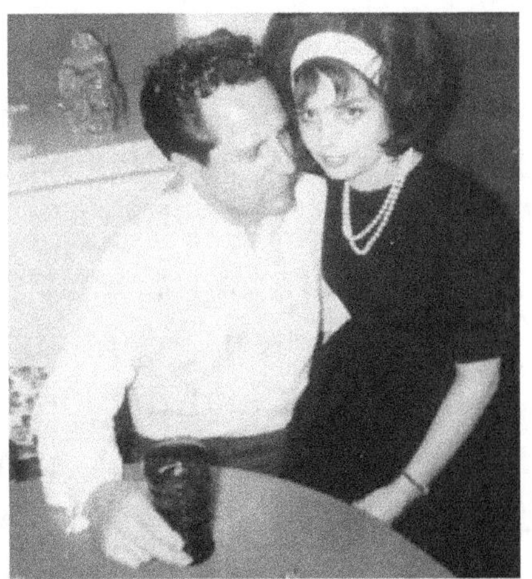

Ladies always loved Hawk

Hawk and Jackie

I heard Ernest Harper say, "If Hawk liked you, you had a friend for life. If he didn't, he would hit you over the head with a cash register." Nuff said…

Hawk rented an old T.V. station on Hwy. 259 between Longview and Kilgore. This place was the berries for a club/cat house combination! He turned the offices into bedrooms and the lobby into a bar room. It had a huge basement where he ran the crap game. The sheriff at that time was Tom Welch. Tom was one of his best customers. This joint was a bust from the get-go!

Russell Tunnel was running the Pines Motel a few miles down the road, and Hawk's "The Silver Slipper" was way too much competition. Russell pulled a few strings with his political connections and had it shut down pretty quick.

Man, my brother and I saw this junk happen nearly every day. We thought it was normal. When the joints would close about 2:00 A.M., everybody would head to an all-night coffee shop in town called the Pickwick Café. The Pickwick was a local spot for all the gangsters in Gladewater after all the night clubs closed.

Reggie told me a story about him and Slim Phillips pulling up in front of the Pickwick about 2:00 in the morning one Saturday in the rain. They saw Sonny Lacey smashing some guy's head into the grille of a '65 Chrysler Imperial. Sonny dropped the guy to the curb and stood up, and he had a pocketknife sticking out of the top of his head. Just another Saturday night at the Pickwick hotel in Gladewater.

Joe Ben got in a beef with some guys one night in this joint and emptied an M-1 carbine into the guy's back windshield. He had filed down the firing pin, and it shot a 30-round clip just like a machine gun. Everybody lived. The police station was right across the street. This was a big stink in town for several days. It took several trips to the D.A.'s office with money in a brown paper sack to get things cooled off.

I remember getting off the school bus many afternoons, and walking in the front door of the My O My Club. Roger Miller would be blaring out of the jukebox, "King of the Road." Sam the Sham and the Pharaohs would rock the house with "Wooly Bully." I would grab a hot BBQ sandwich and bust a couple of racks on the pool table.

Somewhere about '68 or '69, Hawk had got tangled up with fencing a bunch of "hot" money orders. The FBI and Texas Rangers swarmed H & S Auto Sales like gangbusters. They searched the joint, all the trailer houses, the wrecked cars, and any other hiding place they could think of for evidence. The paper trail was not hard to follow. They found money orders from the West Coast all the way to Old Mexico.

The man that broke into the Post Office in Frankston, Texas gave it up and rolled over on Hawk and his accomplices for a lighter sentence. When the smoke cleared, Hawk bought himself ten years in Leavenworth for conspiracy to defraud the federal government. Judge William Wayne Justice of Tyler wrote about it in his memoirs. He wrote, "It was one of the most colorful crimes of open and shut cases he had ever tried."

My brother and I went to the trial at the Federal Court House in Smith County. It took thirty minutes for the judge to read Hawk's rap sheet, dating back to 1945. I just remember Hawk turning himself in the next day to the Smith County Jail. A few days before his trial, Hawk had given Reggie an envelope to pass on to Lindley Beckworth. He was the State Representative for that part of East Texas. A couple of years later Lindley called Reggie to come by his office. He reached in his safe and pulled out that envelope. It had never been opened. Reggie's eyes about popped out when he counted out twenty-five hundred-dollar bills. Hawk was out of options!

Rocky at "the Lake House," 1971

Chapter 9

Reggie and I were on our own after that. I was a senior in high school and Reggie was at Kilgore Junior College. Hawk left in March, and I went to work full-time at an aluminum chair factory in Owentown, Texas. I worked the 3-11 night shift, and went to high school during the day. Reggie was working at the Budweiser beer distributorship in Longview. I don't know how we managed to stay out of jail ourselves.

There was many a wild party held there in 1970. Every parent in town knew where to look for their kids when they didn't come home. Twenty-Two Twelve West Lake Drive was home to many a wayward soul back in the day.

When Hawk left for Leavenworth in April of 1970, Reggie was living in Mesquite, Texas and going to school in Dallas at SMU. A lot of people ask how Reggie was able to afford the tuition at a private school. I always answer with two words—club feet! He was born with no calf muscles, and wore casts and braces to straighten out his feet until he was about five or six years old. When it came time to go to college, his doctor encouraged him to contact the Texas Crippled Children's Association. They checked his medical records, and offered him a free ride to the school of his choice.

Hawk left us with a small frame house on the lake in Gladewater. Hawk had purchased the lake house in about 1968. His good friend, the local Justice of the Peace, Ross Delay, fronted him the money. I think the grand total was $5,000. The house was a two-bedroom frame, painted pink and white, that was located on the west side of Lake Gladewater. Hawk added a couple of bedrooms in to the backside a year later. This was "home, sweet, home!"

Hawk's third wife, Jackie, had promised to hang around, but that only lasted a couple of months until she headed back to Houston. With Reggie gone to Dallas, and Hawk in Kansas, I needed a couple of roommates to help pay the bills.

Charles, John, Ken, and Rocky at the lake house
after high school graduation 1970

John Erwin, James Cowan, and Charles Rhinehart
on a road trip to Villa Acuña, Mexico, 1971

Several classmates of mine and I worked the night shift at an aluminum tubing company in Owentown, Texas. This place was owned by a family from Jerusalem, that paid us $1.80 an hour to work from 3:30 til midnight. This was 20 cents more than the day shift. We made lawn furniture and portable cots for camping. Take-home pay for forty hours was $56.14. It was tough to get up for school every morning, but it kept the bills paid. I remember making many trips to Bossier City, Louisiana on payday. The drinking age was only eighteen at that time. We had money to burn!

Lifelong friends and classmates came the most often, and stayed the longest. It was a freak parade of stoners, beerheads, dropouts, and misfits of all shapes and sizes that dropped in at the lake house for the next two years. The lake house décor was made up of lava lamps, velvet

Elvis paintings, coffee tables made from beer kegs, and a beer sign on every wall.

The first to move in were my friends Raymond and John. A little later, Kenny Kye, Charlie Boy, and J.W. found a temporary home at the lake house at one time or other. We would go to bed at night listening to Jerry Lee Lewis singing, "Drinking Champagne," and wake up listening to Rod Stewart bidding farewell to "Maggie May."

My friend, Raymond, AKA Ray Tay, would dress out at about 225 pounds. He was always instigating a good practical joke, and was game for about any mischievous plan you could put together.

John was the ringleader of our little band of gypsies. He managed to put Raymond through a world of misery the next year and a half that we lived together. You can hear Ray laughing a mile away when he describes some of John's escapades over the years.

Ken Roberts,
Jean Marie Wilkins,
John Erwin, 1972

Ray would have to be at work at about 6 A.M. John was notorious for setting the alarm clock to 3 A.M. just to watch Raymond squeal when he got to work two hours early; or several alarm clocks going off every hour was always good for a few laughs!

After a fun night of heavy partying, John would tape Raymond's ankles together after he was asleep, and yell, "House on fire!" After several bottles of Cold Bear Wine, it was fun to watch Ray roll down the forty-foot embankment out on Highway 271 after he passed out.

John had a quick wit, and a dry sense of humor that still keeps us all laughing forty years later.

John and Tommy Erwin were some of the closest friends we had growing up. Their family fed me and my brother on Christmas Day many times when we had nowhere else to go.

Charlie Boy was built like Johnny Weissmuller, the "Tarzan" movie star. He had a big barrel chest, and was our group's strong man. I remember we had a keg party at

Tommy Erwin and his pet piranha

the lake one night, and Charles was keeping the peace and collecting one dollar from every patron for "all you could drink." A young guy that nobody knew got a black eye from Charlie Boy for calling him a "redneck." The next day, Charles said he laid him out because he thought "redneck" meant that you were gay. New terminology took a while to reach East Texas from the West Coast in 1969.

Kenny Kye was a linebacker for the Gladewater Bears football team. He once bit a guy on the forehead at the bottom of a dog pile, while playing a notorious rival team. Ken was so mean, he wanted to beat up a classmate just for talking in a low, sophisticated voice. I remember him dragging "Worm" Wilson across the front yard for trying to steal an 8-track tape. It was "Carlos Santana's Greatest Hits"!

In my mind's eye, I can still see Kenny in the middle of the dance floor at Ray Martin's Ron-D-Voo Club, doing the "Funky Chicken," wearing a blue leisure suit he bought at Holcombe's Man Shop. Ken could bop with the best of them.

J.W. was our football team's quarterback, and was elected Mr. GHS (Gladewater High School) in 1970. James was a great all-around athlete, and quite the ladies' man. He got a football scholarship to Louisiana Tech University in Ruston, Louisiana. A rumor floated around for years that he was backed up by Terry Bradshaw at quarterback, but Bradshaw got to start after J.W. dropped out after being red-shirted his freshman year.

James made his way back to the lake house every weekend he could, and every holiday. Like the rest of us, J.W. didn't have much of a home life. I remember a merchant from Louisiana calling the house looking for James because he had bought a pair of white patent leather shoes, and written a hot check. When he finally left town, he pitched us the keys to his 1959 Chevy Bel-Air, and said, "She is all yours, boys! Drive her till she pukes."

Not much home cooking took place around the lake house. Many late nights and Sunday dinners were spent at the Shamrock Café. This greasy spoon served a great plate lunch, and a chicken fried steak that would "kill cotton knee high"! It came with a baked spud wrapped in tinfoil, and a dinner salad smothered in homemade garlic dressing. A man could really put on the feed bag at this place.

One of our many common interests was "The King" himself, Elvis Presley. We all were huge fans, and had E.P. playing during each of our weddings. Our lives have scattered out in different directions over the years, but our

Hanging out in Huntsville, Texas with Elvis keeping watch

At the lake house, 1971: Steve Scurlock, Reggie Hawkins, Charles Rhinehart, Rocky Hawkins, James Cowan, John Erwin

Another road trip to Villa Acuña, Mexico, 1971, with Ken Roberts, Reggie Hawkins, Rocky Hawkins, John Erwin, Charles Rhinehart, and "Happy the Clown"

At the lake house, 1972: Mike Alexander, Jim Simmington,
Reggie Hawkins, Barry Cook, Rocky Hawkins, Raymond Murray

friendships have stayed the same. We really helped raise each other, and helped shape one another's lives.

Some of our youthful adventures can't be put to pen and paper because of the statute of limitations hasn't run out yet! Those will be tales for our grandchildren to tell! Crap games and cornbread, poker and pool, a thousand cases of beer with nothing to lose.

After one long night on the town, I managed to knock the fender off of my car on the way home. My roommates came out to inspect the damage. John said, "Don't worry, I can fix it!" He ran in the house, and got a Band-Aid, and slapped it on the wrinkled fender. Raymond unzipped his pants, and "let it rain" on the damage. John said it was the "Miracle Healer." We all busted out laughing, and "popped a top" to seal the deal.

It was not unusual for us to load up and head to Mexico on the spur of the moment. We would drive to Del Rio, Texas, and cross over into Villa Acuña, Mexico. Beer was thirty cents a bottle and you could get a date for $5.00. You could also get your picture put on a book of gopher matches for a dollar. It was the original "Boys Gone Wild!" We made this trip many times, and lived to tell about it. This was the way we rolled in the early 1970s.

You can't go home again, but you can always dream of a time of innocence when we thought we were bulletproof.

If anything good ever came of Hawk's escapades, it gave my brother and me the drive to rise above his old habits.

Reggie graduated from SMU in 1972 with a B.S. in Management and Marketing. I went two years to Kilgore College, and then to Sam Houston State University, where I graduated in 1974 with a degree in Criminal Justice.

After about four and a half years in Leavenworth, Hawk caught a break. Mama Nell, the Madam at a "cat house" in Texarkana, had a good customer that was a State Senator in Arkansas. As a favor to her and her girls, he wrote a letter to the warden in Kansas on Hawk's behalf. He got paroled about six years early. We each graduated about the same time—1974!

Hawk tried to do his parole in Gregg County, but things got a little too hot when a guy called "Rabbit" ended up on the side of the road full of bullet holes in Pritchett,

Texas. Judge Moore put the heat on, and Hawk got his paperwork transferred to Galveston County. This was my last year at Sam Houston, and Reggie had moved in with my roommates and me in Huntsville. It was only a couple of hours from Galveston. Hawk had set up shop in an old joint on the south end of the sea wall called "Tuffy's Bait Camp." Tuffy's was located at the end of the jetties.

Times and the joint had changed ole Hawk quite a bit. He was becoming the "world's oldest hippie"! He had hair down to his shoulders and smoked a lot of weed.

There was not much law enforcement there at all. It was just an old bait house that sold live shrimp, a few supplies, and a lot of beer. Kick open the front door, raise the shutters, and you were in business. About any day of the week, you could catch Hawk and his bay rat friends sitting on a picnic table, blowing a joint, watching the sun go down. We spent many weekends there my senior year. Hawk had an old horse trailer converted over to a camper. He put in two racks of bunk beds and a sink. He screened it in and dragged it up next to the water. It was a good place to crash and get some zzz's!!

Two different hurricanes hit the joint in 1974... completely covered under water. Hawk lived in a 8 x 12 camper next door. He would sweep out the seaweed, and move in a few days later. The place served a mean can of Vienna sausages. My roommates loved this place, and we had one crazy summer.

Hawk had an old cellmate named Jerry Stuart who came to visit one weekend. Jerry had a used car lot and a dealer

Splash Day 1968 in Galveston, Texas, at the Drift Wood Motel
with Rocky Hawkins, John Erwin, Sidney Clinnard,
Charles Rhinehart, and Ken Roberts

license to buy and sell cars. They all ended up at a Cadillac dealership in Houston, and Jerry came home with a new stretch limo, right off the showroom floor. That night he pitched the keys to Reggie, and we hit the sea wall wide open. We made every hot spot in Galveston. I remember riding through the short waves along the beach about sunup with a carload of drunks, all with a huge hangover.

Jerry finally gave it up at Huntsville Penitentiary, doing life for a murder in Kilgore, Texas a few years later. He busted a cap on Pete Boykin with a 12-gauge pump, over a cocaine deal gone bad.

We loved Galveston. About any Splash Day, you could find us at the Drift Wood Hotel on the seawall. We would be

The Lock, Stock, and Barrel in Gladewater, 1986:
Reggie, Rocky, and Glenda Hawkins, and Hawk himself

hanging out on the beach all day, and catching Johnny Winter and the Boogie Kings every night at the Bamboo Hut. Far out!

That last year at Sam Houston, we all hung out at a little neighborhood joint down from campus. It was called "The Lock, Stock, and Barrel." It had swinging doors, a great jukebox, and all the peanuts you could eat, and you were required to throw all the shells on the floor. This was thirty years before Texas Road House. The No. 1 songs that year were, "Stay All Night, Stay A Little Longer," by Willie Nelson, and "Behind Closed Doors," by Charlie Rich. We dropped a many a quarter down the slot to hear those songs in this place. Reggie and I liked this joint so much that we used the namesake and opened our own pizza/pub/restaurant in Longview, Texas in 1978.

Another place we liked to hang out in was called, "The Starting Gate." This was a hole in the wall that seated about 100 people. I saw Willie Nelson there one night for $6.00. He came over to the table and signed an autograph. We had a good visit. I told him about Hawk's stretch in Leavenworth. He wrote,

"Funny How Time Slips Away," and signed his autograph on a napkin for a souvenir. I wish I still had it. I sent it to Hawk. He told me later he swapped it for a pair of sun shades.

Of all the vices Hawk had, he never smoked regular cigarettes. He had to use something else for legal tender, while serving his time.

We opened the Lock, Stock, and Barrel in Gladewater, 1985 and celebrated with an official ribbon cutting.

Restaurant opens for business

A ribbon cutting was held recently for the Lock, Stock and Barrel Restaurant, 1203 W. Marshall. Participating from left were Jim Giles, Les Kroeger, George Nelles, Bill Stoudt Jr., Mary Gott, Bob Maness, Rocky Hawkins, Kelly Louvier, Reggie Hawkins, Jo Ann Hawkins, Guy Harrison, Patteann Daniel, Kathy Rigby and Roy Mozingo.

The original Lock, Stock, and Barrel opened in Longview, Texas in 1979. Bill Stoudt, my old boss (mentioned in the photo caption) is now the County Judge for Gregg County.

Chapter 10

I worked my way through school with many odd jobs. I worked for the City of Gladewater one summer at the Water Department. This was a summer program for dysfunctional families. I also pumped gas at Shaw's Fina Station. I made 75 cents an hour. I didn't have to fix flats, just check the air and pump gas. I sold many gallons for 26 cents. A fill-up cost about five bucks.

I had a '64 Chevy SS Impala that Hawk bought me right before his last trip to Kansas. Man, I kept it spotless while I worked at Shaw's. The station stayed open until 2 A.M. on weekends. Tommy Meeks was the head proprietor when Floyd Shaw was out of town. Tommy would get drunk every Tuesday on his day off, and lock himself in the men's room. He wore glasses that looked like coke bottles, but he was honest and a good man. He taught me everything I know about recycled oil and air pressure. The man could handle a mean swish broom and shammy cloth.

While Tommy Meeks might have been the CEO of Shaw's Fina Station, "Bo" was the general manager in charge of all tire repair. The best I can remember, Bo was about six feet tall, with a big ole barrel chest, and arms like a prize fighter. His head looked like a bowling ball, and was black as midnight. He walked with a limp, and one finger was missing from his left hand. Early in his career, he had a truck tire explode, and hit him between the eyes. This was a 50" spare off a tractor/trailer rig. This slowed Bo down a little, but there was nothing around the station he couldn't handle.

I remember a customer trying to pay Bo with a fifty-dollar bill one night for fixing a flat. Bo refused to take the money, saying a fifty dollar bill was "jankey." I wasn't familiar with the term, and asked him about it later on. He said, "A fifty-dollar bill is jinxed, and would bring you bad luck!" I learned a lot the summer I worked at Shaw's. Every time I see a fifty-dollar bill, I think of Bo and all his wisdom!

One of the more colorful characters that would frequent Shaw's Fina Station was a guy named Billy Applegate. Billy was a part-time roughneck, and a full-time beer drinker. He wore his hair whomped back like Elvis, white shoes, and checkered gabardine pants. He always wore his shirt with the top four buttons open to show off the tattoo on his chest: an ugly reference to the female anatomy. The words *Love* and *Hate*, were inked on each set of his knuckles, and a silver cross dangled from his left ear. Billy always had a good story to tell, and was married to a gal named Pauline. Pauline loved Billy. She had long black hair, and wore "cat-eye" glasses. Somebody said she had a complexion like a peanut patty, and weighed about eighty pounds. I heard

*Billy and
Pauline
Applegate*

E.T. Charles say one time, "She is the only woman I have ever known that can wear baggy stretch pants!" Pauline was good as gold, and had worked in about every café and beer joint in Gladewater at one time or the other.

One summer, I was working for the City street department, and I must have been about sixteen. About a half dozen black dudes and myself were clearing a vacant lot with a weed slinger about 7:30 in the morning. I looked across the street, and saw Billy sitting on the front porch of his house, drinking a 7-oz. bottle of Schlitz Malt Liquor. When our eyes met, Billy hollered out, "Keep up the good work, Rock, that's how I got my start." My soul brothers and I had a good laugh, and Billy had himself another "Baby Bull." (I have used that ole line a thousand times since then, and it always gets a good chuckle from a hard working man.)

One Sunday morning, Billy called E.T. to come bail him out of the city jail; the Cozy Theater had filed charges against Billy Boy for setting off a smoke bomb during the midnight show on a Saturday night. On the way home, E.T. asked him why they thought it was him that set off that smoke bomb, and Billy said, "I don't know, E.T., I think somebody must have seen me!" It was hard not to love Billy!

I left Shaw's when I started to work in Owentown at the aluminum chair factory. When I started Kilgore College, I worked as a fry cook for a while at Long John Silver's. Later on, I got on as a helper at Maxwell Distributing Company. This was the Falstaff/Pearl Beer Distributorship. One summer there, and I graduated to the beer business with R&K Distributors for Budweiser. After graduating from Kilgore College, I headed to Huntsville and the Criminal Justice program at Sam Houston State. I wanted to get into the Probation and Parole department, hoping to help and understand men like my dad. I did work for Gregg County Probation department for awhile.

My time at Sam had me working at a saw mill with a guy named Abel Terriot. This ole guy had a third grade "Cajun Education." He was a self-made millionaire. He got rich recycling used transmission oil and sawdust into floor sweep. He got a contract with the U.S. government, and got rich. He was the largest land owner in Travis County at one time. I got in a bind one weekend over a pool game. Sticks banged off heads and I spent the weekend in the slammer. It was Walker County jail. Abel made my bail, and got me out on Monday, and back to work.

My roommates and I also worked as "yard boys" for a place called Elkins Lake. We did all the mowing and landscaping for this private golf community outside of town on Interstate 45.

I also had a little time working with Piggly Wiggly. It was 1974 and my time was over at Sam Houston State. I didn't have much of a plan, but I had my sheepskin.

Reggie had lived in Huntsville my last couple of semesters, and managed a Pizza Inn. He had worked his way through college, just like me. We both needed some place to call home, so we loaded up and headed back to G-Town after I graduated. We were living by the minute.

We both ended up back in the beer business in Longview. Schlitz Beer Company had just built a new brewery, and we fell in with Stoudt Distributing Company. It was the Schlitz wholesaler. We made many great friends and got to meet people from all different aspects of life. Highway 80 was the "mile of smiles," and we knew every joint owner on a first-name basis.

Hawk had gotten things cooled out with his parole board. He headed back to Gregg County to finish his parole. He scuffled around in the oil patch for a while, recycling drill pipe and hauling junk. He started a little neighborhood gathering every afternoon on a little patch of dirt on Highway 271. Beer and drinks were offered for "donations" only. Hawk was a pretty big novelty for this new generation in Gladewater. As his probation got shorter, his nerve got stronger, and he got the "fix" on to set up shop back out on the strip where he started twenty years earlier.

Site of the Lazy H in recent years

A little, open-air shed metamorphosed into the "Lazy H." Hawk was back in full force. This little, one-room camper evolved into about a half acre of non-stop action.

Hawk got the idea to hang an old car seat up from the rafters like a porch swing; armrest, seat belts and all. I'm sure this came to him in a purple haze of smoke. He built a tin shed, added a bandstand and set twenty-five Lazy Boy recliners front and center. The Axberg Brothers were the headliners at this place—a great band and a bunch of good ole boys. The show was about to begin. There were more car seat swings added, and "smoking" privileges were wide open. Hawkshaw was back! He sold two drinks—Old Milwaukee Longnecks (about 100 cases a week) and one cocktail (a Fuzzy Mother)! This would knock over a stone

*The Axberg Brothers
Band then ...*

... and now

pig! It was a red Solo cup full of Everclear and red punch. He set them on fire for that special ambiance. With a live band, wet t-shirts, no holds barred, he was "catchin' 'em faster than he could string 'em."

The more Hawk smoked, the wilder this place got. He added an old school bus to one end. You could step through the back door of the joint into the bus where a crap game never stopped. The ladies' room was literally in the driver's seat. He removed the seat and installed a toilet. You could drive and do your business at the same time. This was separated from the action by a shower curtain. After a few Fuzzys, nobody cared.

*Domino, King of
the Jungle...
and the Lazy H*

A little later, the old man cut a deal he found in the "Thrifty Nickel Newspaper." It read, "Kitty Needs a New Home." Hawk had a full-grown lion delivered to the property. He was crowned "Domino, King of the Jungle." People came from miles around, just to see if this place was for real! Store hours were from midnight till daylight. When all the other clubs closed down, the place lit up. Hawk ran the dice games—he cut a dollar from the pot every time someone crapped out on the first roll. If the game ran long enough, he would eventually gather up all the money.

When the crap shooters gathered around the dice table you could hear them cry out all kinds of words of encouragement as they tried to make their point. Every number on the dice had a tag line from East Texas. Nearly everyone knew to holler, "Seven come eleven," on their first roll. If a shooter came out with a two or twelve, the line would be, "Snake eyes," or "Box cars." Number three was called, "Ace, deuce, shorty." If a man rolled a four, everybody around the table would holler, "Little Joe from Kokomo!" If five was the point, the tag line might be "Fever in the South, run dice run!" A number six, the cry would be, "Sister Hicks!" Two fours or a five, trey – "Eight, skate, and donate." During World War II, the soldiers around East Texas that were from Wise County, would sing out – "Eighter from Decatur" (Decatur, Texas was about forty miles north of Fort Worth, the county seat of Wise County). Number nine was, "Niner Ross and a Bucking Hoss!" Big ten might be, "Two flowers, five by five," or "Teneha, Tempson, Bobo, and Blair." This tag line originated during the war from the boys living in Shelby County. These were small home towns in East Texas. Some people say when the train ran from Houston to Shreveport, Louisiana, the conductor would be heard loud and clear as he punched out tickets for "Teneha, Tempson, Bobo, and Blair!" Bob Wills had a song out that was a number one hit back in the 1950s using the same line.

Some nights the dice game would go on all night with a ton of money changing hands. Hawk always said, "The more you bet, the more you win!" His wife tended bar, and the band played on! At least for awhile.

Any time there is money being made in the joint business, jealousy and envy will raise its ugly head from your competitors.

The Lazy H was at the top of the list. It was open all night long with no sign of a liquor permit or license to sell alcohol of any kind. Not to mention, open gambling, wet t-shirt contests, and pot smoke so thick you could cut it with a knife. All this put a lot of heat on the local authorities from the other joint operators.

Hawk was paying off the Sheriff, D.A., and the local judge, but the pie was cut up in too many different directions. In 1978, this house of cards came tumbling down. The sheriff was kind enough to send word that the Texas Rangers were in hot pursuit. We were there the night it all came down.

About three o'clock in the morning, the doors flew open, and with lights flashing, guns drawn, Rangers with megaphones warned the patrons they were all under arrest. Glassy-eyed stoners dropped their drinks and lined the walls. Thanks to the tip, Hawk had already grabbed the cash box from the dice table and hit the back door. Some were sent home, but some were sent to jail.

When the smoke cleared, that was the end of the Lazy H Lounge. Hawk tried to relocate in Longview, but the local politics were too much to overcome. He headed out for Mustang Island, south of Corpus Christi.

Hawk, his wife, and his six-year-old stepson hit the road in an old van with a couple of hundred dollars. As usual, all his winnings went to lawyers and politicians for keeping the "fix" on.

Chapter 11

Hawk had always liked the Texas coast. The bay rats, misfits, and laid-back locals fit him to a tee. His connections in Port Aransas were either dead or in jail. But, with a little luck, Hawk happened upon an old realtor hanging a "For Rent" sign in front of a ragged ole café. A fifth of whiskey and twenty percent of the gross, and he was back in business.

He and "Ma Hawkins" swept it out, dragged up a rusted-out barbecue pit out back, and "The Country Bumpkin BBQ" was in business. His business card said, "We Smoke for You Daily." Every time he put a hickory stick on the fire, he lit up a joint for himself. Hawk was the self-proclaimed "World's Oldest Hippie." (He was still tokin' up until about the age of 80!)

His wife, Glenda, was a whole lot smarter than she looked. She was about twenty-five years younger than Hawk, and had lots of ambition. Glad to be gone from South Main Street in Gladewater, she went to work making a business out of nothing. She taught herself how to keep books, applied for a beer license, got loans, did all the banking, and built a good steady clientele on the Island. After a year or two of hard work, a couple of Hawk's ole cronies caught wind of his success, and came down to take a "look-see."

Archie and Norman Grandberry owned a city block in Denver, Colorado. These two ole scufflers from Brownsboro, Texas, had left Gladewater about 1960, with an old jukebox in the trunk of a car, and landed in Denver. They knew how to spread the money around and get the "fix" on! These characters were both pretty smart, and as ruthless as Bonnie and Clyde.

The club downtown was called, "Tricky Dickies," after President Nixon, and "Archie's Round-Up" was a big ole country and western joint outside of town.

Hawk once said, "Archie never needed a floor bouncer in his joints; he could take a can of mace and a slap jack, and clean out a whole joint by himself." His motto was, "Get 'em drunk and get their money." The Grandberrys had a "hat to fit everybody." Politicians and businessmen with credit cards were plentiful for the picking.

They ran a "bust out" joint that was a money-making machine. Fill a joint up with plenty of girls, put a bartender in a bow tie, grab a good loud band, and you were in business. The game plan was to get the girls to sit with the customers, order plenty of champagne cocktails, and get 'em good and drunk. The champagne was nothing, but cold duck wine was about $4 a bottle. One drink was about $7.50, even back then. A lot of the cocktails were recycled from a bucket and resold. It was not unusual at all to bill hundreds of dollars on a credit card —"padding the ticket." No questions were asked because the patrons were guilty of compromising their integrity with mixed company.

There never was any proof that these boys were affiliated with the Dixie Mafia, but they sure got rich in a hurry! Real estate, gambling, and shady investments; they were always on the lookout to hide some cash money. Hawkshaw welcomed them to the beach with open arms. They brought $50,000 in a briefcase when they came to visit.

Archie's connections were "stronger than battery acid." He actually brought the Sheriff of Denver, Colorado with him to Hawk's coming-home party when he got out of Leavenworth. We all sat at our kitchen table and took shots of tequila together!

When Hawk left Mustang Island, he had accumulated a twenty-room hotel, private club, boat storage, souvenir shop, and BBQ joint a la mode. He left it all with the Grandberrys in 1995, including his wife, Glenda.

She finally outgrew ole Hawk. She went to school, got her real estate license, and used all his street sense he had taught her. She ended up married to a drilling rig captain and finally hit the jackpot!

Not long after Ma Hawkins hit the road, ole Hawk headed back to good ole Gladewater. His long time friend, Russell Tunnell, set him up to run the slot machines at his bingo parlor in Tyler, Texas. These "one-armed bandits" paid off in prizes instead of cash.

With a little under-the-table handshake, the prizes could be converted into cash. Hawkshaw was back in business!

Country Bumpkin BBQ and Seahawk Motor Inn,
Mustang Island, Port Aransas, Texas 1979

Like a lot of scams that are illegal, they started off hot, and ran out of gas pretty quick. The state authorities got wise, and created a new law making slots for prizes illegal.

Hawk finally settled down on a little piece of dirt on the outskirts of Gladewater. One of his ole cronies, named Burl Dean Holliman, owned four acres of land outside of town. Hawk moved into an old bread truck that had been converted into a camper. B.D. Holliman never had a clear title to the land, because of back taxes. When he died, he just gave Hawk squatter's rights. Hawk wheeled and dealed for the next fifteen years from this spot. He was keeping a low profile with low overhead. He never looked ahead a single day in his entire life. He scuffled around Trades Day at Canton a few years, but high blood pressure, depression, and diabetes finally took a toll on him.

Right before Hawk checked into the Texan Nursing Home in 2010, the Gregg County police had a warrant out for his arrest for working a guy over with a crescent wrench in a back booth of one of the local cafés in Gladewater. This guy had threatened to burn Hawk out over a car deal gone bad. Hawkshaw was eighty-one years old at the time!

Hawkshaw was a walking contradiction. His personality was a "mystery, wrapped in a riddle." When I was a child, and thought like a child, I figured it was my fault that Hawk never came around. When he had made a big score, and had plenty of money, he would come pick up my brother and me, and every day was like Christmas. When he was broke, we would never see him. It was many years later that I realized that Hawk had a huge inferiority complex, and suffered from depression and low self-esteem, among a long list of psychological defects.

He treated it for years with weed, and a multitude of anti-depressants, from Halcion to Xanax. We had a long discussion once about his need for acceptance and his complex about his treatment of the women in his life. "Everyone has a mother, wife, sister, daughter; no one likes a pimp."

For years, booze shielded him from the pain. Hawk drank an ocean full of Champion Bourbon. Later on it was pot and a variety of prescription meds.

Mostly, it was money that gave him confidence. When he had plenty of it, he knew how to spend it. "Easy come, easy go." Hawk was always generous to a fault, because the money came so easy. Many times I have heard him say, "I have a roll of money a show dog can't jump over." He might also say, "I have enough $100 bills to burn a wet mule." Money was what gave him confidence.

Hawk never saved or invested a penny. He accumulated a house and some land on Highway 42, near the golf course, in White Oak, but later gave it to the lawyers to stay out of jail. He ended up going to jail anyway.

We spent many Christmas and Thanksgiving dinners inside an old beer joint. Hawk would cook for friends and family, and anybody else that might stumble in.

The good times were good, and the bad times were awful. I have dealt with my share of disappointment, fear, and uncertainty. I have since learned that faith, hope, and love can overcome them all.

Bob Dylan said, "The times, they are a-changing," but not for ole Hawk. Every time I go to see him, he is working on a new scam to separate people from their money. Old habits die hard. Hawk will be eighty-six his next birthday.

Epilogue

I lived a crazy, mixed-up life with no direction and no moral compass for the first thirty years of my life.

I penned these few words to say this: "Once, I was lost, but now I am found; blind, but now I see." Jesus Christ reached down to the bottom of life's degradation and saved my soul. Like the apostle Paul said, "Of all the sinners, I am at the top of the list." God is still in the life changing business.

My precious wife and I had a four-year-old son who died of a brain hemorrhage in 1984. It shattered our lives beyond comprehension. There was no amount of money, no political connection, no one to "fix" this heart-breaking circumstance I found myself in.

But, as Wayne Norvelle of First Baptist Church, Gilmer, has said: "When your life is coming unraveled, and you have given up all hope, don't tie a knot in the end of the rope and hang on…let go—and fall into the arms of Jesus!"

My wife was saved as a child and was an active member of the First Baptist Church of Gladewater her whole life. Her pastor at the time of my son's death, Larry Aultman,

In loving memory of
Jacob (Jake) Aaron Hawkins
1980-1984

found out that I was hurting so badly that I could hardly draw a breath. He came over and sat with me on the couch in my mother-in-law's home and read from the Bible three scriptures that would change my life forever:

Romans 8:28

...And we know that in all things God works for the good of those who love Him, who have been called according to His purpose.

II Samuel 12:23

… But now he is dead, wherefore should I fast? Can I bring him back? I shall go to him, but he will not return to me.

John 1:6

Jesus said, "I am the way, the truth, and the life. No man comes to the Father except through me."

First Baptist Church Gladewater bought in an evangelist from Denton, Texas that year. Rick Ingle's testimony changed my life for all eternity the night I attended his service. I will always be grateful to him for being faithful to God's calling. As I look back on my life, and all the mistakes I have made. I thank God every day for the mercy he has had on me!

Anybody who ever heard Hawk tell a story begged him to write a book. He was always too paranoid about who might read it, and get sent back to jail. He often said he was scared he might "talk in his sleep."

Hawkshaw had his own "moral compass." He never indulged in nicotine, never sold drugs, never committed armed robbery. He never used profanity in front of me and my brother; he never laid a hand on us, ever. Uncle Buster always said, "Never do anything illegal, that you can't pay a fine for."

I only caught a glimpse of his escapades, but life is full of memories—some good, some bad—I'm trying to hang on to the good!

Song List

Through the modern miracle of iTunes and YouTube, you can experience the music we enjoyed at the time the events in the book took place. Go ahead, click on your phone and take a musical ride down Memory Lane. It will be fun!

1. "He Ain't Heavy, He's My Brother" — original version by The Hollies, 70s remake by Neil Diamond
2. "Pistol Packin' Mama" — Al Dexter
3. "The Twist" — Chubby Checker
4. "Rainin' in My Heart" — Slim Harpo
5. "Walkin' to New Orleans" — Fats Domino
6. "Return to Sender" — Elvis
7. "Big Blue Diamonds" — Gene Summers
8. "A Change is Gonna Come" — Sam Cooke
9. "Woolly Bully" — Sam the Sham & the Pharaohs
10. "King of the Road" — Roger Miller
11. "Desperados Waiting for a Train" — The Highwaymen (Johnny Cash, Waylon Jennings, Willie Nelson, Kris Kristofferson)
12. "I Walk the Line" — Johnny Cash
13. "Drinking Champagne" — Cal Smith, 70s remake by Jerry Lee Lewis, 90s remake by George Strait
14. "Maggie May" — Rod Stewart
15. "Peace in the Valley" — Elvis
16. "Walkin' in Memphis," "Drift Away," "Lonely Ol' Night," and many more covers by Dennis Ross and the Axberg Brothers Band on YouTube

About the Author

Rocky D. Hawkins and his wife, Laura, live in Gladewater, Texas. He enjoys fishing and coaching Little League Baseball with his grandchildren.

Hawk at Dog Patch, Oklahoma, 1956

(Below, with Loopy the dog)

More Photos

Hawk wheelin' and dealin'

Hawk in New Mexico, 1963

Hawk 1963

E. T. and Lana Charles on their wedding day, 1985

*Hawk
mid-1960s*

*At the Siesta
Motor Courts on
Telephone Road in
Houston, 1964*

John Claude Axberg at the lake house 1975

Orville Ray Griffin, another lake house regular

Danny Hobbs and Barry Cook laughing about the "good old days."

Hawk drove this bread truck conversion camper from Corpus to Gladewater, parked it, and lived there for about 15 years. His needs were very simple.

Wonder how those little boys on the cover turned out?

*Rocky and Reggie Hawkins
at the Crawfish Stand in Big Sandy, Texas, 2015.*

Parole Form No. 18
January, 1937

THE UNITED STATES BOARD OF PAROLE
WASHINGTON, D. C.

Certificate of Conditional Release

Know All Men by these Presents:

It having been made to appear to the United States Board of Parole that

.... Curtis Luke ...., Register No. 512-42 ...., a prisoner

in the ....U.S.Penitentiary, Alcatraz, Calif........., now being entitled to 335 days SGT & 332 days IGT deduction from the term of his sentence, based on commutation for good conduct as provided by Section 1 of the Act of June 21, 1902, Section 2 of the Act of February 26, 1929, and Section 8 of the Act of May 27, 1930, and Amendments thereto, is about to be released in accordance with said Act on the date as determined by the Warden or Superintendent of the said institution, and

WHEREAS, Section 4 of the Act of June 29, 1932, provides that such prisoner shall, upon release, be treated as if released on parole and shall be subject to all provisions of the law relating to the parole of United States prisoners until the expiration of the maximum term or terms specified in his sentence,

Now, THEREFORE, the United States Board of Parole, in accordance with said statute, has decided that the CONDITIONS AS SET FORTH ON THE REVERSE SIDE OF THIS BLANK shall be the conditions under which the said prisoner shall be released, and futhermore, said prisoner shall be subject to such conditions until

......April 14, 1946........which date will be the expiration of the maximum term or terms specified in his sentence, and

BE IT ALSO KNOWN, that this Certificate of Conditional Release does not in any way lessen the obligation of the prisoner to satisfy for payment of fine if such is part of his sentence.

BE IT ALSO KNOWN, that this Certificate of Conditional Release shall not prevent the delivery of the prisoner to authorities of the Federal Government or of any State otherwise entitled to his custody.

Given under the hand and the seal of the said United States Board of Parole this........First........

day of...Febrary..............., Nineteen hundred ...Forty-Three...............

UNITED STATES BOARD OF PAROLE:

ARTHUR D. WOOD, *Chairman*
T. WEBBER WILSON, *Member*
EDWARD P. REIDY, *Member*

By ....WALTER L. UNION........
Parole Executive

By: *L. O. Mills*

L. O. Mills, Acting Parole Officer

UNITED STATES BOARD OF PAROLE:

The above-named prisoner was released on this...1st........day of....February.....................194.3..

.... *J. A. Johnston*........................

J. A. Johnston, *Warden or Superintendent*

Curtis Duke's release papers from Alcatraz

CONDITIONS UNDER WHICH THIS CERTIFICATE OF CONDITIONAL RELEASE IS ISSUED

The following conditions are to become operative immediately:

1. That the said person shall report his arrival at his destination at once on the Arrival Notice provided for that purpose.

2. That he shall, on the last day of each month and at such other times as may be required make a full and truthful written report, on the form prescribed, and shall submit said report to his parole Advisor, who will certify and mail it through the office of the United States Probation Officer to the Supervisor of Parole before the third day of the month following, and that when making his last monthly report previous to the date of maximum expiration as set forth on the face of this certificate, he shall make a full report of his whereabouts and behavior, which shall be considered his final report, unless specifically ordered by the Board of Parole to make a further report.

3. That he will remain within the parole limits fixed by the Board of Parole until the maximum date shown on the face of the certificate, unless permission in writing is given by the Board of Parole to change such limits. To wit:

United States District:........Eastern District Washington - Seattle & Tacoma......................................

4. That if, when released from this institution, he is delivered into the custody of any other United States or State authority, he shall, while in the custody of said authority, send his monthly reports (bearing the attestation of the official under whose direct control his person is) to the Supervisor of Parole through the office of the United States Probation Officer in whose district he is, unless such reports are waived by the Supervisor of Parole. When released from such custody he shall go to the place designated by the Board of Parole and there remain in accordance with the conditions of this certificate.

5. That changes in residence and employment within this district will be made only after written permission therefor is given by the Probation Officer, with the approval of the Supervisor of Parole.

6. That he shall not drink intoxicating liquors, use narcotic drugs, or frequent places where either is sold, dispensed, or used unlawfully.

7. That he shall not associate with persons of bad reputation.

8. That he shall obey all laws and will report direct to his Parole Advisor, his Probation Officer, and to the Supervisor of Parole and any arrest or serious difficulty in which he becomes involved.

9. That his conduct in all respects shall be upright and honorable.

10. That he shall not enter into marriage unless and until written permission therefor has been given by the Supervisor of Parole through the United States Probation Officer.

I hereby certify that I understand the above conditions which have been read and explained to me and under which I am being released.

WITNESS:

....

Curtis Duke   (Prisoner's Signature)

Record Clerk, Leavenworth California ....   Feb. 1, 1943 ....
    (Title)   (Date)

FPI Inc—LK—4-22-40—85M—1079-23